IN A DARK TIME

IN A DARK TIME

edited by

Nicholas Humphrey and
Robert Jay Lifton

faber and faber
LONDON · BOSTON

First published in 1984
by Faber and Faber Limited
3 Queen Square London WC1N 3AU
Set by Goodfellow & Egan Limited Cambridge
Printed in Great Britain by
Whitstable Litho Limited, Whitstable, Kent
All rights reserved

British Library Cataloguing in Publication Data
In a dark time.
1. War – Literary collections
1. Humphrey, Nicholas   II. Lifton, Robert Jay
808.8'0358   PN6071.W35

ISBN 0-571-13362-2
ISBN 0-571-13336-3 Pbk

What if this present were the world's last night?

John Donne

Contents

Introduction

In 1897 the painter Paul Gauguin decided to kill himself.
Before doing so he completed, in a fever of work, his last
great testamentary picture and wrote on it – he said it was
his signature – *D'où venons nous? Que sommes nous? Où
allons nous?* (Where have we come from? What are we?
Where are we going?) Then Gauguin took an overdose of
arsenic. The dose was too large: he vomited it up and
lived.

As a way of solving Gauguin's or any other of life's
riddles, suicide, said Schopenhauer, is a clumsy experiment
to make. For when it succeeds it destroys the very consciousness which asks the question and awaits the answer.
Clumsy or not, the experiment cannot be counted on to
fail. Gauguin himself threw up the arsenic and survived,
but today we live in a world which has been preparing
so long and so carefully for its own experiment in self-
destruction, that when the time comes a successful ending
is virtually assured. If the order comes to go, we go. All
together.

It is in that context that we have put together this book
of writings about the psychological and imaginative confusion which surrounds popular ideas of war, of valour, of
victory over enemies and death. Drawing on the literature
of the last 2,500 years – the work of poets from Sappho to
Robert Lowell, historians from Thucydides to Edward
Thompson, dreamers from St John the Divine to Bob
Dylan – the book pictures human beings at their worst and
at their best: as savage warriors, as helpless victims, as
dupes of 'Nukespeak' and warlike propaganda and, finally,
as individuals who have the courage to say no. It is a book
designed, quite deliberately, as an emetic against war.

But we hope the book is more than that. To Gauguin's

11

three questions there can be only three answers consistent with our survival beyond the nuclear age. Where have we come from? We have come from an antique civilization, led by warriors and shaped by more than 14,000 wars against often illusory enemies, in which we no longer glory. What are we? We are human beings who, in E. P. Thompson's words, at this most critical time in our long history have at last grown up, recognizing that the Other is ourselves. Where are we going? On, and on, as part of the great chain of human being. . . . There are indeed other answers represented in this book, but we leave the reader to discover and to choose among them.

It will be said, with justice, that these answers are not new. People and nations have been sick of war before. They have grandly proclaimed their intention to beat swords into ploughshares, spears into pruning hooks. And yet, those same nations have returned to their old ways within years, if not months, of leaving off.

Today, as we write, the lesson is admitted and depressing. On Armistice Day the citizens of our two countries buy their Flanders poppies, bend their heads before the cenotaphs and wanly commemorate the million soldiers killed in two world wars. But by the month's end the first cruise missiles, each with the power to incinerate a major city, have arrived on European soil. The arsenal is now equivalent to 20,000 million tons of TNT, 1 million Hiroshima bombs – 1,000 tons for every one of the world's rotting soldiers, a poppy for every Hiroshima bomb.

We do not belittle the power of genuine remembrance. Some of the passages in this book are included for no other reason than to keep fresh the horrors of those previous wars and to give voice again to those who at the time resisted them. But in the nuclear age memory alone is not enough. If there is to be a transformation in our attitudes, matching the transformation in the human prospects for survival, we must find ways of *anticipating* the horrors of war on a scale never before realized. We must, as it were, 'launch our imagination on warning', or we shall be too late.

But how to imagine the next war? Einstein said: 'The power set free from the atom has changed everything, except our ways of thinking.' It is true that so many of our imaginative stand-bys are now outdated, so many words and traditions rendered empty, that we hardly know how to begin. Victory – there can be none. Enemies – they are coextensive with our friends. Life after death – there will be no one to remember or succeed us, and the notion of immortality itself is threatened . . . and war – not war but a Nuclear End. As Auden wrote, an 'outrageous novelty' has been introduced into our lives', and now, it seems, 'nothing we learnt before . . . is of the slightest use.' There is no longer anywhere we can be sure of taking our imaginative ground.

Yet, if we are to prevent the Nuclear End, imagine it we must. And here we have to challenge the half-truth hidden within Einstein's truism. In this new situation we do, of course, need radically new ways of thinking. But these new ways must inevitably be founded on the old. We cannot await, and must not expect, some kind of evolutionary mutation of the human mind.

We ourselves do not believe that the answer lies so far away. Progress in human understanding has always depended not so much on tapping sources from another world as on making new use of ideas already close to hand. Human wisdom has been the wisdom of the seer – the poet, painter or peasant revolutionary – who, when the current world view failed, turned the kaleidoscope of his or her imagination until familiar things took on a wholly different pattern. Such can and must be our imaginative strategy now. We are not short of *elemental* images for imagining the End; they are there in the Bible, Shakespeare, Melville, the voices of schoolchildren and, yes, the voices of the politicians. Only the appropriate *form* eludes us, the liberating pattern.

We have tried to begin that formative process in this book. Unlike most anthologies, this is not, in conception, merely a book to be dipped into. Its structure is intended to be closer to a narrative in which neighbouring pieces answer or illuminate each other, and patterns of argument and feeling emerge from the dizzying images. Some pieces have been chosen for their insight into psychology or history, some for their passion, others for their lack of it, and some (including pieces of our own) because they provide linking passages. But they are all there because, in one way or another, they carry the terrible narrative along.

The book attempts to be neither comprehensive nor exhaustive. It is a personal selection, based largely on what was already to hand on the shelves of our studies on either side of the Atlantic. But, given our own professional interests, those shelves inevitably have a special history. One of us, Robert Jay Lifton, is a psychiatrist who has made a close study of human reactions to disaster and loss of identity, notably among victims of the Hiroshima bomb and veterans of the Vietnam war; the other, Nicholas Humphrey, is an experimental psychologist who has been working on the evolution of intelligence and human social consciousness. Although this book is by no means strictly about psychology, it is a psychologically oriented book, bearing the stamp of two editors whose first interest in war and peace lies in the politics, strategies and economics of the human mind rather than the battlefield. To the extent that bookshelves betray the man, it is no accident that we came up with *this* material.

No accident either, given our profession and our cultural background, that there is a certain ideological bias in the selection we have made. Throughout the book the reader will feel – we felt it – a tension between two complementary forces in the life both of the individual and of society, the

14

forces which Freud called the 'death instinct' and the 'life instinct', Thanatos and Eros. We come, as most readers will, of a tradition – the Judaeo-Christian legacy – which for two thousand years has benefited from the cultural expression of this tension between death and life. On the one hand our culture has been dominated by an autocratic, death-dealing God, against whose final judgement there is no appeal. But equally, it has been dominated by an insistence on each individual's responsibility for his or her own fate. For it is the privilege – and the burden – of beings to have knowledge of good and evil and free will: when we come to judgement we come to it *on our own account,* according to how we have lived our earthly lives.

It has been the achievement of Judaeo-Christian culture, at its best, to keep these twin philosophies creatively in balance. The meaning of life lay in its relation to death. Now, however, the balance is disturbed. We are offered redemption – a claim to meaning – for carrying out the unredeeming, meaningless act of extinguishing ourselves as a civilization, and perhaps as a species, by our own hand with our own tools. 'There is a land where contrarieties are equally true,' William Blake wrote in his poem 'Milton'. But with the advent of the atomic bomb, the acceptance of contrarieties has become a dangerous illusion. 'The US must possess the ability to wage nuclear war rationally,' said a British-born US Defense adviser in 1982. One of the morals we draw from our own history is that that particular contrariety stops here.

The book opens with a section on *words*. 'Words', as Aldous Huxley says in a passage from a previously unpublished speech which bears on everything that follows, 'form the channel along which thought flows . . . where peace and war are concerned, most people use the wrong words. . . . The result is that they see reality through a distorting medium. Often they don't see it at all.' Nowhere is this more obvious than in people's attitudes to *enemies* (section 2): 'All political and nationalistic propaganda aims at only one thing; to persuade one set of people that another set of people are not really human and that it is therefore legitimate to rob, swindle, bully and even murder them.' Faced with illusory enemies, people let go of moral standards, and *civilization in suspense* (section 3) leaves space for the emergence of psychotic fantasies and an immersion in the imagery of death. Then, as Rebecca West wrote, we see that *only part of us is sane* (section 4); and, most sinisterly, given the present possibility of total world destruction, such fantasies of death and dying can become turned against the self and merge with an apocalyptic vision. But while images of a cleansing and immortalizing holocaust fail to confront the essential *nothingness* of the Nuclear End (section 5), on another level the truer, nightmare vision does break through: '*There's a nuclear war going on inside me,*' says a child interviewed at a school in Brookline, Massachusetts (section 6) – for children and adults alike, fears for the future are undermining human trust, stunting personal development and leading to a general psychic numbing. With numbness comes the *abandonment of hope* (section 7), but, as the last two sections show, there are other reactions and another way: *in a dark time, the eye begins to see.*

All this, of course, is itself no more than another book of words, a record of some of the channels along which sane and insane thoughts have flowed. But books and words are what we have and what we leave behind. If anything in our culture symbolizes the fact and hope of human continuity, it is the continuing presence of the poets, philosophers and thinkers of the last few thousand years who, in the service of life, once stretched their imagination and can now stretch ours. We would have included those ancestral voices anyway, but we summon them now not least because this fight for human survival is as much their fight as ours. If we go, they go.

But we do not believe it has to happen. And if it does not happen, the reason may be that the preparations for mass suicide have already gone too far. You can fool some of the people some of the time, but the accumulation of destructive weaponry is now so great that people, ordinary people the world over, are beginning to rebel.

Gauguin wrote of his picture: 'Before dying I put into it all my energy, a passion so painful in terrible circumstances, and a vision so clear . . . that life surges up.' This book too was in some ways a painful work to put together. We hope that through it life surges up.

N.K.H.
R.J.L.
January 1984

1

Words

On the pavement
of my trampled soul
the soles of madmen
stamp the prints of rude, crude, words.

Vladimir Mayakovsky, 'I', 1912

⟱⟰

I speak to you tonight as a man of letters – a man whose profession it is to deal with words. Words, you will say, words – what have words to do with peace? The answer is that they have a great deal to do, not only with peace, but with everything else. Words are the instruments of thought; they form the channel along which thought flows; they are the moulds in which thought is shaped. If we wish to think correctly it is essential that we should use the appropriate words. . . . Now, it seems to me, that where peace and war are concerned, most people use the wrong words. They use words which do not describe the facts of the contemporary situation. Indeed they use words which actually conceal those facts. The result is that they see reality through a distorting medium. Often they don't see it at all. . . .

Let me give you a concrete example: In a recent speech, the Archbishop of Canterbury made the following remark – 'The use of force, of the sword, by the State, is the ministry of God for the protection of the people.' Consider this sentence carefully. The two key words in it are 'force' and 'sword'. Of these, the first is an empty abstraction, having as it stands, no definite meaning of any kind. The second is a picturesque anachronism. The sword – it is a fine word. It suggests chivalry; it calls up visions of knights in shining armour. All very nice and cultured and reassuring.

But let us translate the Archbishop's vague, misleading verbiage into words which express the concrete facts of contemporary reality. 'The use of force by the State, that is to say the use of fire bombs, mustard gas and high explosives dropped by aeroplanes upon defenceless civil populations, is the ministry of God for the protection of the people.' Put in these words it doesn't sound quite so good. We begin to have certain doubts about 'the ministry of God for the protection of the people'. . . .

The same applies equally well to such noble and consoling phrases as sanctions, collective security, international police force and the like. Translate these abstractions – and you will find that what is really being talked about is always the same thing. War – war waged with modern scientific weapons. Behind the screen of polite, lying words are tanks and planes and mustard gas. . . .

Or consider another example. We constantly speak of human beings in ways which implicitly deny their humanity – in words which reduce them to being mere representatives of a class, mere symbolical representations of some principle. Bourgeois, Bolshevik, Fascist, Communist. . . . Not one of these words describes the concrete reality of the men and women to whom it is applied. Not one of them but is used by the speakers to arouse an unjustified hatred or an equally unjustified pride and vanity. And what is the effect of this upon our thoughts and feelings and actions? The effect is disastrous. Most people would hesitate to torture or kill a human being like themselves. But when that human being is spoken of as though he were not a human being, but as the representative of some wicked principle, we lose our scruples. All political and nationalistic propaganda aims at only one thing; to persuade one set of people that another set of people are not really human and that it is therefore legitimate to rob, swindle, bully and even murder them. To achieve this end, propagandists always make use of the same device;

they teach people to think of their fellow men and women in terms of unsuitable words.

Aldous Huxley, speech delivered at the Albert Hall, London, 1936

❖⟫∘⟪❖

> They held up a stone.
>   I said, 'Stone.'
> Smiling they said, 'Stone.'
>
> They showed me a tree.
>   I said, 'Tree.'
> Smiling they said, 'Tree.'
>
> They shed a man's blood.
>   I said, 'Blood.'
> Smiling they said, 'Paint.'
>
> They shed a man's blood.
>   I said, 'Blood.'
> Smiling they said, 'Paint.'

Dannie Abse, adapted from the Hebrew of Amir Gilboa, 1982

❖⟫∘⟪❖

There was, then, civil conflict; and the cities . . . pushed on to further extremes of innovation both in the ingenuity of their schemes for seizing power and in the extravagance of their reprisals. They altered the accepted usage of words in relation to deeds as they thought fit. Reckless audacity was termed courageous loyalty to party; prudent hesitation, specious cowardice; moderation, a cover for spinelessness; and ability to understand all sides, total inertia. Fanatical enthusiasm was rated a man's part; and cautious deliberation, a euphemism for desertion.

Thucydides, *The Peloponnesian War*, III, 83, 5th century BC

'We sterilize the area prior to the insertion of the Revo-lutionary Development team,' says the colonel.

Mary McCarthy, *Report from Vietnam*, 1967

The background linguistic system of each language is not merely a reproducing instrument for voicing ideas but rather is itself a shaper of ideas, the program and guide for the individual's mental activity, for his analysis of impressions, for his synthesis of his mental stock in trade. . . . We dissect nature along lines laid down by our native languages. The categories and types that we isolate from the world of phenomena we do not find there because they stare every observer in the face; on the contrary, the world is presented in a kaleidoscope of impressions which has to be organized by our minds – and this means largely by the linguistic systems in our minds. We cut nature up, organize it into concepts, and ascribe significances as we do, largely because we are parties to an agreement to organize it in this way – an agreement which holds through our speech community and is codified in the patterns of our language. The agreement is, of course, an implicit and unstated one, BUT ITS TERMS ARE ABSOLUTELY OBLIGATORY; we cannot talk at all except by subscribing to the organiz-ation and classification of data which the agreement decrees.

Benjamin Lee Whorf, *Language, Thought and Reality*, 1956

How many men aboard each chopper?
Five of us. And we landed next to the village, and we all got on line and we started walking toward the village. And there was one man, one gook in the shelter, and he was all huddled up down in there, and the man called out and said there's a gook over there.

How old a man was this? I mean was this a fighting man or an older man?
An older man. And the man hauled out and said there's a gook over here, and then Sergeant Mitchell hollered back and said shoot him.

Interview with Vietnam veteran, *New York Times*,
25 November 1969

Lastly, stood War, in glittering arms yclad,
    With visage grim, stern looks, and blackly hued;
In his right hand a naked sword he had,
    That to the hilts was all with blood imbrued;
    And in his left, that kings and kingdoms rued,
        Famine and fire he held, and therewithal
        He razed towns and threw down towers and all.

Cities he sacked and realms, that whilom flowered
    In honour, glory, and rule above the best,
He overwhelmed and all their fame devoured,
    Consumed, destroyed, wasted, and never ceased,
    Till he their wealth, their name, and all oppressed;
        His face forhewed with wounds, and by his side
        There hung his targe, with gashes deep and wide.

In midst of which, depainted there, we found
  Deadly Debate, all full of snaky hair,
That with a bloody fillet was ybound,
  Out-breathing nought but discord everywhere.

> Thomas Sackville, Earl of Dorset, 'The Shield of War',
> *c.* 1600

There is 'great rejoicing at the nation's capital'. So says the
  morning's paper.
The enemy's fleet has been annihilated.
Mothers are delighted because other mothers have lost
  sons just like their own;
Wives and daughters smile at the thought of new-made
  widows and orphans;
Strong men are full of glee because other strong men are
  either slain or doomed to rot alive in torments;
Small boys are delirious with pride and joy as they fancy
  themselves thrusting swords into soft flesh, and
  burning and laying waste such homes as they
  themselves inhabit;
Another capital is cast down with mourning and
  humiliation just in proportion as ours is raised up,
  and that is the very spice of our triumph . . .
This is life – this is patriotism – this is rapture!
But we – what are we, men or devils? and our Christian
  capital – what is it but an outpost of Hell?

> Ernest H. Crosby, 'War and Hell', 1898 (at the outbreak of
> the Spanish-American War)

BLESSING OR CURSE? One of the greatest scientific discoveries in the history of mankind was announced yesterday – how to release the almost unlimited energy of the atom. *Daily Worker*, 7 August 1945

A message from the *Augusta* late this afternoon states that Mr Truman personally made the announcement about the bomb to officers of the *Augusta* in the wardroom. He said, 'The experiment has been an overwhelming success.'
The Times, 7 August 1945

The fundamental power of the universe, the power manifested in the sunshine that has been recognized from the remotest ages as the sustaining force of earthly life, is entrusted at last to human hands.
The Times, 8 August 1945

BIG NAVY BASE GETS NO. 2
Daily Worker, 10 August 1945

Since yesterday, we have been learning from a mob of enthusiastic commentators that now any middle-sized city can be totally obliterated by a bomb the size of a football. The American, English and French newspapers are spewing out elegant dissertations on the atomic bomb. We can sum it up in a single phrase: mechanized civilization has just achieved the last degree of savagery. . . . Already it is hard enough to breathe in this tortured world. But now we are being offered a new form of anguish, which may well be final. . . . Perhaps, after all, it does provide the pretext for a special edition of the newspapers. But that edition should be full of silence.

Albert Camus, 'Combat', 8 August 1945

Speak, you also,
speak as the last,
have your say.

Speak –
But keep yes and no unsplit,
And give your say this meaning:
give it the shade.

Give it shade enough,
give it as much
as you know has been dealt out between
midday and midday and midnight.

Look around:
look how it all leaps alive –
where death is! Alive!
He speaks truly who speaks the shade.

Paul Celan, 'Speak, You Also', 1980

The United States must possess the ability to wage nuclear war rationally.

Colin Gray, US Defense Department consultant, 1982

A man may take to drink because he feels himself to be a failure, and then fail all the more completely because he drinks. It is rather the same thing that is happening to the English language. It becomes ugly and inaccurate because our thoughts are foolish, but the slovenliness of our language makes it easier for us to have foolish thoughts.

George Orwell, 'Politics and the English Language', 1946

We have . . . learned to live with the unthinkable and to think it. Last spring, I saw people, not superficially psychotic-looking, wearing T-shirts with 'Nuke Buenos Aires' on the front. A new verb, 'to nuke'. So easily, in such an unacknowledged way, has the unthinkable slipped into our vocabulary. Note, too, how 'to nuke' is an active verb; it is easier to think of killing than of being killed, for obvious reasons. Can such atrocious garments be donned on Albion's shore without an enraged populace tearing them from the wearers' backs? They can.

The rational, objective arguments against Britain's participation in the scenario for blasting non-combatants off the earth in the name of military strategy and for subsequently rendering the planet uninhabitable have been deployed again and again, with increasing force, over the last three decades. And this is the result of it; the Argies have only so much as to tweak the lion's tail and pow! How easily the final solution slips out! That the British do not have the capacity to unilaterally 'nuke' Buenos Aires is beside the point. The ease with which this neologism springs to the lips of the pro-nuclear lobby is unnerving in itself. There is a little man walks up and down the airport lobby in Boston, Massachusetts, carrying a hand-painted sign: 'Nuke Jane Fonda'.

Angela Carter, 'Anger in a Black Landscape', 1983

❦

When people are deeply uneasy about what and how much to feel, the specific call to feel what happens on the other end of a nuclear weapon is not a very inviting one. . . . Rather than feel the weapons' malignant actuality, we render them benign. In calling them 'nukes', we render them small and 'cute', something of the order of a household pet. That tendency was explicit in the naming of the two atomic bombs dropped on Japanese cities – the first 'Little Boy' suggesting a newborn baby, the second 'Fat Man' after Winston Churchill. Even Japanese survivors domesticated their bomb by referring to it with the not-unpleasant-sounding term *pikadon*, or 'flash-boom'. . . .

What are we to make of terms like 'nuclear exchange', 'escalations', 'nuclear yield', 'counterforce', 'megatons', or of 'the window of vulnerability' or (ostensibly much better) 'window of opportunity'. Quite simply, these words provide a way of talking about nuclear weapons without really talking about them. In them we find nothing about billions of human beings being incinerated or literally melted, nothing about millions of corpses. Rather, the weapons come to seem ordinary and manageable or even mildly pleasant: a 'nuclear exchange' sounds something like mutual gift giving.

Robert Jay Lifton, *Indefensible Weapons*, 1982

Nukespeak is not the product of a concerted propaganda effort to rewrite dictionaries. It is more subtle, more pervasive, and probably unconscious, though none the less effective for that. It would be rash to think that a critical awareness of Nukespeak alone could change anything about the processes that give rise to the military industrial complex and nuclear politics. But it can contribute to change by increasing our awareness of the extent to which Western culture is intertwined with notions of nuclear violence; it can provide a means whereby people can begin to retake control of their own language and exchange their own meanings and values. . . . There is certainly no substitute for facts and arguments based on them, but what must be recognized is that there are no 'facts' or 'arguments'

Words

---

in public discussion that are not selected, defined or dressed
up by the devious devices of human language.

Paul Chilton, 'Nukespeak', 1982

Back and forth, back and forth
goes the tock, tock, tock
of the orange, bland, ambassadorial
face of the moon
on the grandfather clock.

All autumn, the chafe and jar
of nuclear war;
we have talked our extinction to death.
I swim like a minnow
behind my studio window.

Our end drifts nearer,
the moon lifts,
radiant with terror.
The state
is a diver under a glass bell.

A father's no shield
for his child.
We are like a lot of wild
spiders crying together,
but without tears.

Nature holds up a mirror.
One swallow makes a summer.
It's easy to tick
off the minutes,
but the clockhands stick.

Back and forth!
Back and forth, back and forth –
my one point of rest
is the orange and black
oriole's swinging nest!

Robert Lowell, 'Fall 1961', 1961

⋖➣◦➢⋗

If, on account of the political situation,
There are quite a number of homes without roofs, and men
Lying about in the countryside neither drunk nor asleep,
If all sailings have been cancelled till further notice,
If it's unwise now to say much in letters, and if,
Under the subnormal temperatures prevailing,
The two sexes are at present the weak and the strong,
That is not at all unusual for this time of year.
If that were all we should know how to manage. Flood, fire,
The desiccation of grasslands, restraint of princes,
Piracy on the high seas, physical pain and fiscal grief,
These after all are our familiar tribulations,
And we have been through them all before, many, many
                                                times.
As events which belong to the natural world where
The occupation of space is the real and final fact
And time turns round itself in an obedient circle,
They occur again and again but only to pass
Again and again into their formal opposites,
From sword to ploughshare, coffin to cradle, war to work,
So that, taking the bad with the good, the pattern composed
By the ten thousand odd things that can possibly happen
Is permanent in a general average way.

32

Till lately we knew of no other, and between us we
seemed
To have what it took – the adrenal courage of the tiger,
The chameleon's discretion, the modesty of the doe,
Or the fern's devotion to spatial necessity:
To practise one's peculiar civic virtue was not
So impossible after all; to cut our losses
And bury our dead was really quite easy: That was why
We were always able to say: 'We are children of God,
And our Father has never forsaken His people.'

But then we were children: That was a moment ago,
Before an outrageous novelty had been introduced
Into our lives. Why were we never warned? Perhaps we
were.
Perhaps that mysterious noise at the back of the brain
We noticed on certain occasions – sitting alone
In the waiting room of the country junction, looking
Up at the toilet window – was not indigestion
But this Horror starting already to scratch Its way in?
Just how, just when It succeeded we shall never know:
We can only say that now It is there and that nothing
We learnt before It was there is now of the slightest use,
For nothing like It has happened before. It's as if
We had left our house for five minutes to mail a letter,
And during that time the living room had changed places
With the room behind the mirror over the fireplace;
It's as if, waking up with a start, we discovered
Ourselves stretched out flat on the floor, watching our
shadow
Sleepily stretching itself at the window. I mean
That the world of space where events re-occur is still there,
Only now it's no longer real; the real one is nowhere
Where time never moves and nothing can ever happen:
I mean that although there's a person we know all about
Still bearing our name and loving himself as before,

33

That person has become a fiction; our true existence
Is decided by no one and has no importance to love.

W. H. Auden, 'For the Time Being: A Christmas
Oratorio', 1942

I start with Incomprehension, where I suspect many of us
both begin and end. . . . For I do not see how any human
being whose intelligence and sensitivities have been shaped
by traditional facts and values could possibly understand
the nature of these unnatural, other-worldly weapons. So-
called 'facts' about the Bomb are not facts in the ordinary
sense at all: they are not facts we can relate to, get our
minds round. Mere numbers, words.

Let me repeat a fact. The bomb which was dropped on
Hiroshima killed 140,000 people. The Uranium it contained
weighed about twenty-five pounds; it would have packed
into a cricket ball. 140,000 people is about equal to the
total population of Cambridge.

I cannot grasp that kind of fact. I cannot make the
connection between a cricket ball and the deaths of everyone who lives in Cambridge. . . . And when someone
tells me – and I tell you – that a war between the United
States and Russia will now mean a Second World War
every second, and that the equivalent of 5,000 Hiroshima
bombs will land in England, my imagination draws a
blank. It is not just that I cannot *bear* the thought: I cannot
even *have* the thought of 5,000 Hiroshima bombs. . . .

We close off from such nonsense. Try as we may, we
shall not get the message. Our minds are minds finely
tuned by culture and by evolution to respond to the
frequencies of the real world. And when a message comes
through on an alien wavelength it sets up no vibrations.

The so-called facts pass clean through us and away, like radio emissions from the stars.

There are strange and interesting precedents in history. When Captain Cook's great ship, the *Endeavour*, sailed two hundred years ago into Botany Bay, the Australian aborigines who were fishing off the shore showed *no* reaction. 'The ship' – I quote from Joseph Banks' journal of the voyage – 'passed within a quarter of a mile of them and yet they scarce lifted their eyes from their employment . . . expressed neither surprise nor concern.' In the experience of these people nothing so monstrous had ever been seen upon the surface of the waters – and now it seems they could not see it when it came.

But theirs was a selective blindness. Cook put down his rowing boats: *now* the natives were alarmed, now they looked to their defences. Blind to the greater but incomprehensible terror, they reacted quick enough to a threat which came within their ken.

We too react, selectively, to man-sized threats. It is not giant dangers or giant tragedies, but the plight of single human beings which troubles us. In a week when 3,000 people are killed in an earthquake in Iran, a lone boy falls down a well-shaft in Italy – and the whole world grieves. Six million Jews are put to death in Hitler's Germany, and it is Anne Frank trembling in her garret that remains stamped into our memory.

The story of Hiroshima too can be told as the story of individual human beings. The tale, for example, of a little girl: 'When my grandmother came back, I asked "Where's Mother?" "I brought her on my back," she answered. I was very happy and shouted "Mama!" But when I looked closely, I saw she was only carrying a rucksack. I was disappointed. . . . Then my grandmother put the rucksack down and took out of it some bones. . . . I miss my mother very much.'

Keiko Sasaki and her mother. But multiply the tragedy

a hundred thousand times, and it no longer has any meaning to us. We are each too human to understand the killing power of nuclear weapons, each too close to the good earth to understand how a metal cricket ball could explode with the force of ten thousand tons of TNT. Each of us aboriginally blind.

We must live with this blindness. It will not change. I do not expect my dog to learn to read *The Times*, and I do not expect myself or any other human being to learn the meaning of nuclear war, or to speak rationally about megadeaths or megatonnes of TNT. The most we can ask for is an open recognition that neither we, when we protest against nuclear armaments, nor the generals and politicians when they defend them, know what we are talking about.

Nicholas Humphrey, 'Four Minutes to Midnight', 1981

The neutron weapon is for Western Europe today what the English longbow was for Henry V and his army at Agincourt in 1415.

Daily Express, 10 August 1981

The man on television, Sunday midday, middle-aged and solid, nice-looking chap, all the facts at his fingertips, more dependable looking than most high-school principals, is talking about civilian defense, his responsibility in Washington. It can make an enormous difference, he is saying. Instead of the outright death of eighty million American citizens in twenty minutes, he says, we can, by careful planning and practice, get that number down to only forty million, maybe even twenty. . . . The thing to do, he says, is to evacuate the cities quickly and have everyone shelter in the countryside. That way we can recover, and meanwhile we will have retaliated, incinerating all of Soviet society, he says. What about radioactive fallout? he is asked. Well, he says. Anyway, he says, if the Russians know they can only destroy forty million of us instead of eighty million, this will deter them. Of course, he adds, they have the capacity to kill all two hundred and twenty million of us if they were to try real hard, but they know we can do the same to them. If the figure is only forty million this will deter them, not worth the trouble, not worth the risk. Eighty million would be another matter, we should guard ourselves against losing that many all at once, he says.

If I were sixteen or seventeen years old and had to listen to that, or read things like that, I would want to give up listening and reading. I would begin thinking up new kinds of sounds, different from any music heard before, and I would be twisting and turning to rid myself of human language.

Lewis Thomas, *Late Night Thoughts on Listening to Mahler's Ninth Symphony*,1983

I know you:
You are light as dreams,
Tough as oak,
Precious as gold,
As poppies and corn,
Or an old cloak:
Sweet as our birds

To the ear,
As the burnet rose
In the heat
Of Midsummer:
Strange as the races
Of dead and unborn:
Strange and sweet
Equally,
And familiar,
To the eye,
As the dearest faces
That a man knows,
And as lost homes are:
But though older far
Than oldest yew –
As our hills are, old –
Worn new
Again and again:
Young as our streams
After rain:
And as dear
As the earth which you prove
That we love.

Edward Thomas, 'Words', 1920

GOTCHA!

Headline in the *Sun* following the sinking of the
Argentinian battleship, *General Belgrano*,
with the loss of more than 300 lives. 4 May 1982.

2

Enemies

All that most maddens and torments; all that stirs up the lees of things; all truth with malice in it; all that cracks the sinews and cakes the brain; all the subtle demonisms of life and thought; all evil, to crazy Ahab, were visibly personified, and made practically assailable in Moby Dick. He piled upon the whale's white hump the sum of all the general rage and hate felt by his whole race from Adam down; and then, as if his chest had been a mortar, he burst his hot heart's shell upon it.

Herman Melville, Moby Dick, 1851

✥◦✥

Once a nation bases its security on an absolute weapon, such as the atom bomb, it becomes psychologically necessary to believe in an absolute enemy.

Patrick Blackett, President of the Royal Society, 1956

✥◦✥

The man beside me was saying, 'We have a different regard for human life than those monsters do.' He was referring to what he said was the Soviets' belief in winning nuclear war despite casualties that we would find unacceptable. And he added that they are 'godless' monsters. It is this theological defect 'that gives them less regard for humanity or human beings'. The man telling me all this was Ronald Reagan, as I interviewed him [in 1980] on a flight from Birmingham to Orlando.

Robert Scheer, With Enough Shovels, 1982

✥◦✥

The threat of an enemy – even recourse to war – has always afforded to uneasy rulers a means of internal ideological regulation and social discipline. This was a familiar notion to Shakespeare. The dying Henry IV, knowing that the succession was beset with enemies, advised his son –

> Therefore, my Harry,
> Be it thy course to busy giddy minds
> With foreign quarrels.

This advice led Henry V to Agincourt.

The threat of the Other is grounded upon a profound and universal human need. It is intrinsic to human bonding. We cannot define whom 'we' are without also defining 'them' – those who are not 'us'. 'They' need not be perceived as threatening: they may be seen only as different from 'us' – from our family, our community, our nation: 'they' are others who do not 'belong'. But if 'they' are seen as threatening to us, then our own internal bonding will be all the stronger. . . . Rome required barbarians, Christendom required pagans, Protestant and Catholic Europe required each other. Patriotism is love of one's own country; but it is also hatred or fear or suspicion of others. . . .

[Today] the Western hemisphere has been divided into two parts, each of which sees itself as threatened by the Other; yet at the same time this continuing threat has become necessary to provide internal bonding and social discipline within each part. Moreover, this threat of the Other has been internalized within both Soviet and American culture, so that the very self-identity of many American and Soviet citizens is bound up with the ideological premises of the Cold War.

Edward Thompson, *Beyond the Cold War*, 1982

The men of Gilead said unto him, Art thou an Ephraimite? If he said, Nay; then said they unto him, Say now Shibboleth: and he said Sibboleth: for he could not frame to pronounce it right. Then they took him, and slew him at the passages of Jordan; and there fell at that time of the Ephraimites forty and two thousand.

Judges 12: 5–6

◆⊃∘⊂◆

As soon as the Europeans had recovered from the shock of their defeat [by Batu Khan in 1241] they turned to thoughts of reprisal. Pope Gregory IX preached a crusade against the Mongol terrorists. In order to support the thesis that any form of barbarity would be justifiable in such a holy cause it was proclaimed that 'The Mongol princes who had dogs heads ate the bodies of the dead leaving only the bones to the vultures . . . the old and ugly women were divided into daily portions for the common folk while the pretty young women, having been ravished, had their breasts torn open and were then reserved as titbits for the grandees. . . .' [But] we now know that the dog-headed cannibals against whom Pope Gregory IX preached his crusade were representatives of a far more sophisticated civilization than anything that existed in Europe at that time.

Edmund Leach, *Custom, Law and Terrorist Violence*, 1977

◆⊃∘⊂◆

Dr Narut's naval work appeared to involve establishing how to induce [US] servicemen who might not be naturally inclined to kill to do so under certain circumstances. . . . The idea is to get the men to think of the potential enemies they will have to face as inferior forms of life. They are given lectures and films which portray personalities and customs in foreign countries whose interests may go against the USA. The films are biased to present the enemy as less than human: the stupidity of local customs is ridiculed, local personalities are presented as evil demigods, rather than as legitimate political figures.

Peter Watson, *War on the Mind*, 1980

❦

Instructions issued to the German Press, February, April, 1943:

Stress: If we lose this war, we do not fall into the hands of some other states but will all be annihilated by world Jewry. Jewry firmly decided to exterminate all Germans. International law and international custom will be no protection against the Jewish will for total annihilation.

Stress: In the case of the Jews there are not merely a few criminals (as in every other people), but all of Jewry rose from criminal roots, and in its very nature is criminal. The Jews are no people like other people, but a pseudo-people welded together by hereditary criminality.

❦

I am told that, moved by some foolish urge, they [the Christians] consecrate and worship the head of a donkey, that most abject of all animals. This is a cult worthy of the customs from which it sprang! Others say that they reverence the genitals of the presiding priest himself, and adore them as though they were their fathers'. . . . As for the initiation of new members, the details are as disgusting as they are well-known. A child, covered in dough to deceive the unwary, is set before the would-be novice. The novice stabs the child to death with invisible blows; indeed he himself, deceived by the coating of dough, thinks his stabs harmless. Then – it's horrible! – they hungrily drink the child's blood, and compete with one another as they divide his limbs. . . . Precisely the secrecy of this evil religion proves that all these things, or practically all, are true.

A pagan's view of Christian practices,
Minucius Felix, 'Octavius', 3rd century

These Scythian husbandmen then occupy the country eastward, for three days' journey. . . . Beyond this region the country is desert for a great distance; and beyond the desert [in the region around Moscow] the Androphagi dwell. . . . The Androphagi have the most savage customs of all men; they pay no regard to justice, nor make use of any established law. They . . . speak a peculiar language; and of these nations, are the only people that eat human flesh.

Herodotus, *Histories* 243; 272–3, 5th century BC

Both [sides] already have the capacity to destroy each other's population many times over. But a continuing arms race with all its dangers is better than accepting an imbalance which would leave us at the mercy of the cold-blooded murderers of Sakhalin.

The Times, leading article, following the shooting down of a Korean airliner, 5 September 1983

Every so often [Gallup Polls] ask their respondees to select from a list of adjectives the ten which best describe members of other nations. . . . Back in 1942, Germany and Japan were our bitter enemies, and Russia was our ally; and in 1942, among the first five adjectives chosen to characterize both the Germans and the Japanese were: 'warlike', 'treacherous', and 'cruel'. None of these appeared in the list for the Russians at that time. In 1966, when Gallup surveyed responses to mainland China, predictably, the Chinese were seen as 'warlike', 'treacherous', and, being Orientals, 'sly'. After President Nixon's visit to China, however, almost immediately these adjectives disappeared about the Chinese, and they are now characterized as 'hard-working', 'intelligent', 'artistic', 'progressive', and 'practical'.

Jerome D. Frank, 'Prenuclear-age leaders
and the nuclear arms race', 1982

❦

The man who loves and serves his own community is the one best qualified to serve the rest of mankind. We are here this afternoon to celebrate not only the Red Army but Russian patriotism. . . . We are living through the greatest and most critical days in human history. The Red Army stands astride the whole continent of Europe as the guardian of civilization. The great heart of unconquerable Russia, the deep love of her children for their country, their skill, their devotion, their daring, their valour, their disregard of every motive except the single one of driving out the Hun – those are the things which bar the eastward road of Germany to world domination. We and the allied nations, and their sons in arms who represent them here, bar the other roads to the south and west. We too have taken our punishment in this grim struggle: probably we have much more still to take. But the example of the Red Army – its resilience after long retreat and painful disaster – is a living encouragement to us to push on: until, against the greatest crime in history – and the greatest criminal – is saved the future commonwealth of mankind.

A. V. Hill, Member of Parliament for Cambridge University and Nobel Prize-winner, speech in London, February 1942

O wad some Pow'r the giftie gie us
To see oursels as others see us!
It wad frae mony a blunder free us,
    And foolish notion.

Robert Burns, 'To a Louse', *c*. 1786

This terrifying power which nobody and nothing can check is mostly explained as fear of the neighbouring nation, which is supposed to be possessed by a malevolent fiend. Since nobody is capable of recognizing just where and how much he is himself possessed and unconscious, he simply projects his own condition upon his neighbour, and thus it becomes a sacred duty to have the biggest guns and the most poisonous gas. The worst of it is that he is quite right. All one's neighbours are in the grip of some uncontrollable fear, just like oneself. In lunatic asylums it is a well-known fact that patients are far more dangerous when suffering from fear than when moved by rage or hatred.

C. G. Jung, 'Psychology and Religion', 1937

I opened my eyes in daylight. My head was roughly bandaged, and the man with the withered arm was watching my face. . . . 'We found you at dawn,' said he, 'and there was blood on your forehead and lips. . . . You believe now that the room is haunted?' He spoke no longer as one who greets an intruder, but as one who grieves for a broken friend.

'Yes,' said I, 'the room is haunted.'

'Tell us, is it truly the old earl . . . ?'

'No,' said I, 'it is not. . . . There is neither ghost of earl or ghost of countess in that room, there is no ghost there at all; but worse, far worse . . . the worst of all the things that haunt poor mortal man . . . and that is, in all its nakedness – *Fear!* Fear that will not have light nor sound, that will not bear with reason, that deafens and darkens, and overwhelms. It followed me through the corridor, it fought against me in the room. . . .'

H. G. Wells, 'The Red Room', 1896

For many years we have suckled on fear and fear alone, and there is no good product of fear. Its children are cruelty and deceit and suspicion germinating in our darkness. And just as surely as we are poisoning the air with our test bombs, so are we poisoned in our souls by fear, faceless, stupid sarcomic terror.

John Steinbeck, *Once There Was a War*, 1958

Had he and I but met
By some old ancient inn,
We should have sat us down to wet
Right many a nipperkin!

But ranged as infantry,
  And staring face to face,
I shot at him as he at me,
  And killed him in his place.

I shot him dead because –
  Because he was my foe,
Just so: my foe of course he was:
  That's clear enough; although

He thought he'd 'list, perhaps,
  Off-hand like – just as I –
Was out of work – had sold his traps –
  No other reason why.

Yes; quaint and curious war is!
  You shoot a fellow down
You'd treat if met where any bar is,
  Or help to half-a-crown.

Thomas Hardy, 'The Man He Killed', 1902

He who hath slain his thousands in the fray
Should shed hot tears, and celebrate the day
With funeral rites, such as wan mourners pay.

Lao-Tzu, 6th century BC

I felt sorry. I don't know why I felt sorry. John Wayne
never felt sorry.

American infantryman remembering feelings after killing
a Vietnamese guerrilla with a knife, 1974

49

We have all read what happened between those two oppos-
ing armies, and how it came unexpected, undesigned, and
yet willed with all the unconscious force of their natures.
Not once or twice but again and again we hear of this
sudden change upon the night of Christmas Eve, how
there was singing upon one side answered by the other,
and how the men rose and advanced to meet each other as
if they had been released from a spell. Everyone who tells of
it speaks also of his own wonder as if he had seen a miracle;
and some say that the darkness became strange and beautiful
with lights as well as music, as if the armies had been
gathered together there not for war but for the Christmas
Feast. Our men, as if from mere habit, began to sing,
Christians Awake! And then the Christian did awake in
English and in German, and they were no longer German or
English to each other, but men. It was not done by an
effort or with fear and suspicion and awkwardness. It
happened as if it were a change of weather, the sun coming
out after a storm; and when it happened it seemed more
natural even than wonderful. What was unnatural was the
former state of war in which men had been to each other
not men but targets; and now they had come to life for
each other, and in a moment they were friends.

A. Clutton-Brock, 'Christmas 1914'

At this moment a man, presumably carrying a message to
an officer, jumped out of the trench and ran along the top
of the parapet in full view. He was half-dressed and was
holding up his trousers with both hands as he ran. I
refrained from shooting at him. It is true that I am a poor
shot and unlikely to hit a running man at a hundred
yards. . . . Still, I did not shoot partly because of that
detail about the trousers. I had come here to shoot at

'Fascists'; but a man who is holding up his trousers isn't a 'Fascist', he is visibly a fellow creature, similar to yourself, and you don't feel like shooting at him.

George Orwell, *Homage to Catalonia*, 1938

⊲⊃∘⊂⊳

In 1957 at the Labour Party's debate on disarmament, Aneurin Bevan declared that he was not prepared to 'go naked into the conference chamber'. . . . But what was it that Bevan had to hide? Bevan came into the world naked, naked he left it. Why should he have been afraid to go naked into the conference chamber to discuss matters of global life and death? What he had to hide, as much from himself as from his adversaries, was nothing less than his humanity.

Of course, by the rules of the game he had to hide it. For no naked human being, conscious of his own essential ordinariness, the chair seat pressing against his buttocks, his toes wriggling beneath the conference table, his cock hanging limply a few feet from Mr Brezhnev's, could play the game of international politics and barter like a god with the lives of millions of his fellow men. No naked human being could threaten to press the nuclear button.

So I come to my proposal. Our leaders must be given no choice but to go naked into the conference chamber. At the United Nations General Assembly, at the Geneva disarmament negotiations, at the next summit in Moscow or in Washington, there shall be a notice pinned to the door. 'Reality gate. Human beings only beyond this point. NO CLOTHES.' And then, as the erstwhile iron maiden takes her place beside the erstwhile bionic commissar, it may dawn on them that neither she nor he is made of iron or steel but rather of a warmer, softer and much more magical material, flesh and blood. Perhaps as Mr Brezhnev looks at his navel and realizes that he, like the rest of us, was once joined from there to a proud and aching mother, as Mrs Thatcher feels the table-cloth tickling her belly, they will start to laugh at their pretensions to be super-human rulers of the lives of others. If they do not actually make love they will, at least, barely be capable of making war.

Nicholas Humphrey, 'An Immodest Proposal', 1982

◈⊃◦⊂◈

'They are coming,' he whispered. 'They will take over the meadows where we pitch our tents. They will organize torchlight parades. They will build rostrums and fill them, and down from the rostrums they will preach our destruction'. . . .

Have you ever seen a rostrum from behind? All men and women – if I may make a suggestion – should be familiarized with the rear view of a rostrum before being called upon to gather in front of one. Everyone who has ever taken a good look at a rostrum from behind will be immunized *ipso facto* against any magic practised in any form whatsoever on rostrums. Pretty much the same applies to the rear view of church altars; but that is another subject.

Günter Grass, *The Tin Drum*, 1959

◈⊃◦⊂◈

Why this sudden bewilderment, this confusion?
(How serious people's faces have become.)
Why are the streets and squares emptying so rapidly,
everyone going home lost in thought?

Because night has fallen and the barbarians haven't come.
And some of our men just in from the border say
there are no barbarians any longer.

Now what's going to happen to us without barbarians?
Those people were a kind of solution.

> C. P. Cavafy, 'Waiting for the Barbarians', 1975

❖⊃∘⊂❖

The French will only be united under the threat of danger.
No one can simply bring together a country that has 265
kinds of cheese.

> Charles de Gaulle, speech, 1951

❖⊃∘⊂❖

The logic of killing others in order to affirm our own life
unlocks much that puzzles us in history, much that with
our modern minds we seem unable to comprehend, such
as the Roman arena games. If the killing of a captive
affirms the power of your life, how much does the actual
massive staging of life–and–death struggles affirm a whole
society? The continual grinding sacrifice of animal and
human life in the arenas was all of a piece with the
repressions of a society that was dedicated to war and that
lived in the teeth of death. . . . The more death you saw
unfold before your eyes and the more you thrust your
thumbs downward, the more you bought off your own
life. . . . The longer people looked at the death of someone else, the more pleasure they could have in sensing the
security and the good fortune of their own survival.

The whole meaning of a victory celebration . . . is that
we experience the power of our lives and the visible
decrease of the enemy: it is a sort of staging of the whole

meaning of war – which is why the public display, humiliation, and execution of prisoners is so important. 'They are weak and die: we are strong and live.' The Roman arena games were, in this sense, a continued staging of victory even in the absence of a war; each civilian experienced the same powers that he otherwise had to earn in war. If we are repulsed by the bloodthirstiness of those games, it is because we choose to banish from our consciousness what true *excitement* is.

Ernest Becker, *Escape from Evil*, 1975

I must kill my visible enemy, the one who is determined to take my life, to prevent him from killing me. Killing gives me a feeling of relief, because I am dimly aware that in killing him, I have killed death. My enemy's death cannot be held against me, it is no longer a source of anguish, if I killed him with the approval of society: that is the purpose of war. Killing is a way of relieving one's feelings, of warding off one's own death.

Eugene Ionesco, 'Journal', 1966

3

Civilization in Suspense

We are mad, not only individuals, but nations also. We restrain manslaughter and isolated murders; but what of war and the so-called glory of killing whole peoples? Our greed has no limit, nor our cruelty. When crimes are committed stealthily by individuals they are less harmful and less monstrous; but deeds of cruelty are done every day by command of senate and popular assembly, and servants of the state are ordered to do what is forbidden to the private citizen. The same deeds which would be punished by death if committed in secret are applauded when done openly by soldiers in uniform. Man, the gentlest of animals, is not ashamed to glory in blood-shedding and to wage war when even the beasts are living in peace together.

Seneca, *Letters* XCV, 1st century

⊷⊂⊃∘⊂⊐⊶

Sir,
Against the vast majority of my countrymen, even at this moment, in the name of humanity and civilization, I protest against our share in the destruction of Germany.

A month ago Europe was a peaceful comity of nations; if an Englishman killed a German he was hanged. Now, if an Englishman kills a German, or if a German kills an Englishman, he is a patriot, who has deserved well of his country. We scan the newspapers with greedy eyes for news of slaughter, and rejoice when we read of innocent young men, blindly obedient to the word of command, mown down in thousands by the machine-guns of Liège. Those who saw the London crowds during the nights leading up to the Declaration of War saw a whole population, hitherto peaceable and humane, precipitated in a few days down the steep slope of primitive barbarism, letting loose, in a moment, the instincts of hatred and

57

blood lust against which the whole fabric of society has been raised. 'Patriots' in all countries acclaim this brutal orgy as a noble determination to vindicate the right; reason and mercy are swept away in one great flood of hatred; dim abstractions of unimaginable wickedness – Germany to us and the French, Russia to the Germans – conceal the simple fact that the enemy are men, like ourselves, neither better nor worse – men who love their homes and the sunshine, and all the simple pleasures of common lives; men now mad with terror in the thought of their wives, their sisters, their children, exposed, with our help, to the tender mercies of the conquering Cossack.

And all this madness, all this rage, all this flaming death of our civilization and our hopes, has been brought about because a set of official gentlemen, living luxurious lives, mostly stupid, and all without imagination or heart, have chosen that it should occur rather than that any one of them should suffer some infinitesimal rebuff to his country's pride. . . .

And behind the diplomatists, dimly heard in the official documents, stand vast forces of national greed and national hatred – atavistic instincts, harmful to mankind at its present level, but transmitted from savage and half-animal ancestors, concentrated and directed by Governments and the Press, fostered by the upper class as a distraction from social discontent, artificially nourished by the sinister influence of the makers of armaments, encouraged by a whole foul literature of 'glory', and by every text-book of history with which the minds of children are polluted.

Bertrand Russell, letter to the *Nation*, London,
15 August 1914

Cruelty has a Human Heart,
And Jealousy a Human Face;
Terror the Human Form Divine,
And Secrecy the Human Dress.

The Human Dress is forged Iron,
The Human Form a fiery Forge,
The Human Face a Furnace seal'd,
The Human Heart its hungry Gorge.

William Blake, 'The Divine Image', 1794

Archetypes are like river beds which dry up when the water deserts them, but which it can find again at any time. An archetype is like an old water-course along which the water of life has flowed for centuries, digging a deep channel for itself. The longer it has flowed in this channel the more likely it is that sooner or later the water will return to its own bed. The life of the individual as a member of society and particularly as part of the State may be regulated like a canal, but the life of nations is a great rushing river which is utterly beyond human control. . . . Thus the life of nations rolls on unchecked, without guidance, unconscious of where it is going, like a rock crashing down the side of a hill, until it is stopped by an obstacle stronger than itself. Political events move from one impasse to the next, like a torrent caught in gullies, creeks and marshes. All human control comes to an end when the individual is caught in a mass movement. Then the archetypes begin to function, as happens also in the lives of individuals when they are confronted with situations which cannot be dealt with in any of the familiar ways.

C. G. Jung, 'Wotan', 1936

The September Massacres [Paris, 1792] have been viewed, and properly so, as an example of the phenomenon called 'revolutionary neurosis', in which there occurs a complete breakdown of those instincts and restraints that keep at a deep and usually harmless level the maniacal forces that flow beneath human consciousness. Just as an individual, subjected to certain inner pressures beyond his endurance, will suddenly go mad and destroy himself and those around him, so too, apparently, can a segment of society take leave of its senses and deliver itself to the forces of destruction. . . .

The massacres began on the afternoon of September 2 . . . and went on for five more days and nights. On the morning of the third, the prison of La Force was entered, and here took place the murder of the Princesse de Lamballe. . . . The frenzy of the crazed and drunken murderers appears to have reached its highest pitch at La Force. Cannibalism, disembowelment and acts of indescribable ferocity took place there. The Princess, a timid but loyal spirit, had returned to France from the safety of England to be by the side of her friend Marie Antoinette during the troubled days of 1792. She had been arrested in the Temple Tower, where she had accompanied the royal family in its imprisonment, and was returned to La Force, where she met her end a few weeks later. Brought before Maillard's 'tribunal', she refused to swear her hatred of the King and Queen, and was duly handed over to the mob. She was dispatched with a pike thrust, her still beating heart was ripped from her body and devoured, her legs and arms were severed from her body and shot through cannon. The horrors that were then perpetrated on her disemboweled torso are indescribable; traditionally they have remained cloaked in the obscurity of medical Latin.

Stanley Loomis, *Paris in the Terror: June 1793 –
July 1794*, 1965

❦❀❦

[This war] disregards all the restrictions known as International Law, which in peacetime the states had bound themselves to observe; it ignores the prerogatives of the wounded and the medical service, the distinction between civil and military sections of the population, the claims of private property. It tramples in blind fury on all that comes in its way, as though there were to be no future and no peace among men after it is over.

Peoples are more or less represented by the states which they form, and these states by the governments which rule them. The individual citizen can with horror convince himself in this war of what would occasionally cross his mind in peacetime – that the state has forbidden to the individual the practice of wrongdoing, not because it desires to abolish it, but because it desires to monopolize it, like salt and tobacco. A belligerent state permits itself every such misdeed, every such act of violence, as would disgrace the individual. It makes use against the enemy not only of the accepted *ruses de guerre*, but of deliberate lying and deception as well – and to a degree which seems to exceed the usage of former wars. The state exacts the utmost degree of obedience and sacrifice from its citizens, but at the same time it treats them like children by an excess of secrecy and a censorship upon news and expressions of opinion which leaves the spirits of those whose intellects it thus suppresses defenceless against every unfavourable turn of events and sinister rumour. It absolves itself from the guarantees and treaties by which it was bound to other states, and confesses shamelessly to its own rapacity and lust for power, which the private individual has then to sanction in the name of patriotism.

It should not be objected that the state cannot refrain from wrongdoing, since that would place it at a disadvantage. It is no less disadvantageous, as a general rule, for the individual man to conform to the standards of morality and refrain from brutal and arbitrary conduct; and the state seldom proves able to indemnify him for the sacrifices it exacts. Nor should it be a matter for surprise that this relaxation of all the moral ties between the collective individuals of mankind should have had repercussions on the morality of individuals; for our conscience is not the inflexible judge that ethical teachers declare it, but in its origin is 'social anxiety' and nothing else. When the community no longer raises objections, there is an end, too, to the suppression of evil passions, and men perpetrate deeds of cruelty, fraud, treachery and barbarity so incompatible with their level of civilization that one would have thought them impossible.

Well may the citizen of the civilized world . . . stand helpless in a world that has grown strange to him.

Sigmund Freud, 'Thoughts for the Times on War and Death', 1915

❖❖❖

It may be several weeks or even months before I shall ask you to drench Germany with poison gas, and if we do it, let us do it one hundred per cent. In the meanwhile, I want the matter studied in cold blood by sensible people and not by that particular set of psalm-singing uniformed defeatists which one runs across now here and there.

Winston Churchill, secret memorandum, 6 July 1944

❖❖❖

There are no rules in [this] game. Hitherto acceptable norms of human conduct do not apply. If the US is to survive, longstanding American concepts of 'fair play' must be reconsidered. We must develop effective espionage and counterespionage services and must learn to subvert, sabotage and destroy our enemies by more clever, more sophisticated, and more effective methods than those used against us. It may become necessary that the American people be made acquainted with, understand and support this fundamentally repugnant philosophy.

Report of the United States Hoover Commission, 1950

❦

And what is war, what is needed for success in war, what are the morals of the military world? The object of warfare is murder; the means employed in warfare – spying, treachery, and the encouragement of it, the ruin of a country, the plunder of its inhabitants . . . trickery and lying, which are called military strategy; the morals of the military class – absence of all independence, that is, discipline, idleness, ignorance, cruelty, debauchery, and drunkenness.

Leo Tolstoy, *War and Peace*, 1872

❦

The unique psychological processes which the individual undergoes in Basic Training have been well identified. . . . The early weeks of training are characterized by physical and verbal abuse, humiliation, and a constant discounting and discrediting of everything in which the recruit believes and everything which serves to characterize him as an individual. His head is shaved, his ability to think independently is scorned, and every moment of his day is minutely programmed and scheduled. Even his accustomed language pattern must be renounced, and college graduates are reduced under the taunts of sarcastic drill sergeants to a vocabulary of monosyllabic conformity interspersed with obscenities adopted from their mentors. . . .

Military training and particularly Basic Training embody

the concrete realization of attitudes and activities that are diametrically opposed to the practice and spirit of democracy. Obedience, the keystone of military order, is incompatible with the candid expression of opinion and the right to question and critically examine courses of action, prerogatives that are inherent in the role of mature citizens in a democracy. Obedience instilled in Basic Training leads effectively to dependence with a reliance upon and acceptance of the will of others. Responsibility for one's own welfare and for the consequences of one's acts is relinquished and remains habitually in the hands of superiors.

Peter G. Bourne, 'From Boot Camp to My Lai', 1971

Today we have naming of parts. Yesterday,
We had daily cleaning. And tomorrow morning,
We shall have what to do after firing. But today,
Today we have naming of parts. Japonica
Glistens like coral in all of the neighbouring gardens,
    And today we have naming of parts.

This is the lower sling swivel. And this
Is the upper sling swivel, whose use you will see,
When you are given your slings. And this is the piling
                                                    swivel,
Which in your case you have not got. The branches
Hold in the gardens their silent, eloquent gestures,
    Which in our case we have not got.

This is the safety-catch, which is always released
With an easy flick of the thumb. And please do not let me
See anyone using his finger. You can do it quite easy
If you have any strength in your thumb. The blossoms
Are fragile and motionless, never letting anyone see
    Any of them using their finger.

And this you can see is the bolt. The purpose of this
Is to open the breech, as you see. We can slide it
Rapidly backwards and forwards: we call this
Easing the spring. And rapidly backwards and forwards
The early bees are assaulting and fumbling the flowers:
    They call it easing the Spring.

They call it easing the Spring: it is perfectly easy
If you have any strength in your thumb: like the bolt,
And the breech, and the cocking-piece, and the point of
                           balance,
Which in our case we have not got; and the almond-
                         blossom
Silent in all of the gardens and the bees going backwards
                      and forwards
    For today we have naming of parts.

                    Henry Reed, 'Naming of Paris', 1946

Soldiers killed in two World Wars:

Country	1914–18	1939–45
France	1,363,000	202,000
Germany	2,037,000	3,250,000
Great Britain	723,000	557,000
Italy	460,000	149,000
Japan	n.a.	1,507,000
Russia/USSR	1,700,000	7,500,000
United States	126,000	292,000
Worldwide	**8,418,000**	**16,933,000**

Whereasthe Congressoftheunitedstates byaconcurrent-resolutionadoptedon the4thdayofmarch lastauthorizedthe Secretaryofwar to cause to be brought to theunitedstates-the body of an American whowasamemberoftheamerican-expeditionary force in europe who lost his life during the worldwarandwhoseidentityhasnotbeenestablished for burial inthe memorialamphitheatreof the national cemetery at-arlingtonvirginia

In the tarpaper morgue at Châlons-sur-Marne in the reek of chloride of lime and the dead, they picked out the pine box that held all that was left of

enie menie minie moe plenty other pine boxes stacked up there containing what they'd scraped up of Richard Roe

and other person or persons unknown. Only one can go. How did they pick John Doe?

Make sure he ain't a dinge, boys.

make sure he ain't a guinea or a kike,

how can you tell a guy's a hundredpercent when all you've got's a gunnysack full of bones, bronze buttons stamped with the screaming eagle and a pair of roll puttees?

. . . and the gagging chloride and the puky dirtstench of the yearold dead . . .

The day withal was too meaningful and tragic for applause. Silence, tears, songs and prayer, muffled drums and soft music were the instrumentalities today of national approbation.

John Dos Passos, *Nineteen Nineteen*, 1912

❧◦☙

Well, there've always been people going around saying someday the war will end. I say, you can't be sure the war will *ever* end. Of course it may have to pause occasionally

– for breath, as it were – it can even meet with an accident
– nothing on this earth is perfect – a war of which we could
say it left nothing to be desired will probably never exist.
A war can come to a sudden halt – from unforeseen causes
– you can't think of everything – a little oversight, and the
war's in the hole, and someone's got to pull it out again!
The someone is the Emperor or the King or the Pope.
They're such friends in need, the war has really nothing to
worry about, it can look forward to a prosperous future.

Bertolt Brecht, *Mother Courage*, 1938

Over the empty fields a black kite hovers,
   And circle after circle smoothly weaves.
In the poor hut, over her son in the cradle
   A mother grieves:
'There, suck my breast: there grow and take our bread,
And learn to bear your cross and bow your head.'

Time passes. War returns. Rebellion rages.
   The farms and villages go up in flame,
And Russia in her ancient tear-stained beauty,
   Is yet the same,
Unchanged through all the ages. How long will
The mother grieve and the kite circle still?

Alexander Blok, 'The Kite', 1918

'I'm cold,' Snowden said softly. 'I'm cold.'
   'You're going to be all right, kid,' Yossarian reassured
him with a grin. 'You're going to be all right.'
   'I'm cold,' Snowden said again in a frail, childlike voice,
'I'm cold.'

'There, there,' Yossarian said, because he did not know what else to say. 'There, there. . . .'

'I'm cold,' Snowden whimpered. 'I'm cold.'

'There, there,' Yossarian mumbled mechanistically in a voice too low to be heard. 'There, there.'

Yossarian was cold, too, and shivering uncontrollably. He felt goose pimples clacking all over him as he gazed down despondently at the grim secret Snowden had spilled all over the messy floor. It was easy to read the message in his entrails. Man was matter, that was Snowden's secret. Drop him out of a window and he'll fall. Set fire to him and he'll burn. Bury him and he'll rot like other kinds of garbage. . . .

'I'm cold,' Snowden said. 'I'm cold.'

'There, there,' said Yossarian. 'There, there.' He pulled the rip cord of Snowden's parachute and covered his body with the white nylon sheets.

'I'm cold.'

'There, there.'

Joseph Heller, *Catch 22*, 1955

◈⋙◦⋘◈

It was a war between two races of ants, the red always pitted against the black, and frequently two red ones to one black. The legions of these Myrmidons covered all the hills and vales in my wood-yard, and the ground was already strewn with the dead and dying, both red and black. It was the only battle which I have ever witnessed, the only battle-field I ever trod while the battle was raging; internecine war; the red republicans on the one hand, and the black imperialists on the other. On every side they were engaged in deadly combat, yet without any noise that I could hear, and human soldiers never fought so resolutely. I watched a couple that were fast locked in each other's embraces, in a little sunny valley amid the chips, now at noonday prepared to fight till the sun went down, or life went out. The smaller red champion had fastened himself like a vise to his adversary's front, and through all the tumblings on that field never for an instant ceased to gnaw at one of his feelers near the root. . . . They fought with more pertinacity than bulldogs. Neither manifested the least disposition to retreat. It was evident that their battle-cry was 'Conquer or die.' I should not have wondered by this time to find that they had their respective musical bands stationed on some eminent chip, and playing their national airs the while, to excite the slow and cheer the dying combatants. I was myself excited somewhat as if they had been men . . . . I have no doubt that it was a principle they fought for . . . and not to avoid a three-penny tax on their tea; and the results of this battle will be as important and memorable to those whom it concerns as those of the battle of Bunker Hill. . . .

I never learned which party was victorious, nor the cause of the war; but I felt for the rest of the day as if I had had my feelings excited and harrowed by witnessing the struggle, the ferocity and carnage, of a human battle before my door. . . . The battle which I witnessed took place in the Presidency of Polk.

Henry Thoreau, *Walden*, 1854

4

Only Part of Us is Sane

Only part of us is sane: only part of us loves pleasure and the longer day of happiness, wants to live to our nineties and die in peace, in a house that we built, that shall shelter those who come after us. The other half of us is nearly mad. It prefers the disagreeable to the agreeable, loves pain and its darker night despair, and wants to die in a catastrophe that will set life back to its beginnings and leave nothing of our house save its blackened foundations. Our bright natures fight in us with this yeasty darkness, and neither part is commonly quite victorious, for we are divided against ourselves and will not let either part be destroyed. This fight can be observed constantly in our personal lives. There is nothing rarer than a man who can be trusted never to throw away happiness, however eagerly he sometimes grasps it. In history we are as frequently interested in our own doom. Sometimes we search for peace, sometimes we make an effort to find convenient frontiers and a proper fulfilment for racial destinies; but sometimes we insist on war, sometimes we stamp into the dust the only foundations on which we can support our national lives. We ignore this suicidal strain in history because we are constantly bad artists when we paint ourselves.

Rebecca West, *Black Lamb and Grey Falcon*, 1942

Little Johnny Jones
He was a US pilot,
And no shrinking vi'let
Was he.
He was mighty proud
When World War Three
Was declared,
He wasn't scared,
No siree!
And this is what he said on
His way to Armageddon:

So long, mom,
I'm off to drop the bomb,
So don't wait up for me.
But though I may roam,
I'll come back to my home,
Although it may be
A pile of debris.
Remember, mommy,
I'm off to get a commie,
So send me a salami,
And try to smile somehow.
I'll look for you
When the war is over,
An hour and a half from now.

Tom Lehrer, 'So Long, Mom', 1965

❖

I have had the happiest possible life, and have always been working for war, and have now got into the biggest in the prime of life for a soldier. . . . Thank God, we are off in an hour. Such a magnificent regiment! Such men, such horses! Within ten days I hope Francis and I will be riding side by side straight at the Germans.

Riversdale Grenfell, 1915

❖

The great moment had come. The curtain of fire lifted from the front trenches. We stood up. We moved in step, irresistibly, towards the enemy lines. I was boiling with a mad rage which had taken hold of me and all the others in an incomprehensible fashion. The overwhelming wish to kill gave wings to my feet. The monstrous desire for annihilation which hovered over the battlefield thickened the brains of men in a red fog. We called each other in

74

sobs, and stammered disconnected sentences. A neutral observer might have perhaps believed we were seized by an excess of happiness.

Ernst Jünger, *Diary*, 1918

⁂

Our unconscious, then, does not believe in its own death; it behaves as if it were immortal . . . [It] knows nothing that is negative, and no negation; in it contradictories coincide. . . . This may be the secret of heroism.

Sigmund Freud, 'Thoughts for the Times on War and Death', 1915

⁂

The sense of immortality is much more than a mere denial of death, though man is certainly prone to that denial; it is part of compelling, life-enhancing imagery, through which each of us perceives his connection with all of human history. The sense of immortality may be expressed biologically, that is by living on through or in one's sons and daughters (or, via an expanding biosocial radius, in one's community, nation, people or species); theologically, in the idea of a life after death or, more importantly, of the spiritual conquest of death; creatively, through works and influences, large or small, that persist beyond biological death; through identification with 'external nature' and its infinite extension into time and space; or through a feeling-state of 'experiential transcendence' – so intense that time and death disappear.

The warrior's courage in killing becomes associated with one or more of these modes, so that his immortality, his glory, becomes Everyman's.

Robert Jay Lifton, *Home from the War*, 1974

⁂

If God were to take one or the other of us, I should go and live in Paris.

Samuel Butler, *Notebooks*, 1912

✧⇒◦⇐✧

Suicide may also be regarded as an experiment – a question which man puts to Nature, trying to force her to answer. The question is this; What change will death produce in a man's existence and in his insight into the nature of things? It is a clumsy experiment to make, for it involves the destruction of the very consciousness which puts the question and awaits the answer.

Arthur Schopenhauer, 'On Suicide', 1851

✧⇒◦⇐✧

To die must be an awfully big adventure.

J. M. Barrie, *Peter Pan*, 1904

✧⇒◦⇐✧

If I commit suicide, it will not be to destroy myself but to put myself back together again. Suicide will be for me only one means of violently reconquering myself, of brutally invading my being, of anticipating the unpredictable approaches of God. By suicide, I reintroduce my design in nature. I shall for the first time give things the shape of my will.

Antonin Artaud, 'On Suicide', 1965

✧⇒◦⇐✧

He shut himself up in his cell and stripped himself naked . . . and took his scourge with the sharp spikes, and beat himself on the body and on the arms and on the legs, till blood poured off him as from a man who has been cupped. One of the spikes on the scourge was bent crooked, like a hook, and whatever flesh it caught it tore off. He beat himself so hard that the scourge broke into three bits and the points flew against the wall. He stood there bleeding and gazed at himself. It was such a wretched sight that he was reminded in many ways of the appearance of the beloved Christ, when he was fearfully beaten. Out of pity for himself he began to weep bitterly. And he knelt down, naked and covered in blood, in the frosty air, and prayed to God to wipe out his sins from before his gentle eyes.

Friar Heinrich Suso, description of his own self-flagellation,
c. 1300

No more painters, no more writers, no more musicians, no more sculptors, no more religions, no more royalists, no more imperialists, no more anarchists, no more socialists, no more Bolsheviks, no more politicians, no more proletarians, no more democrats, no more armies, no more police, no more nations, no more of these idiocies, no more, no more, NOTHING, NOTHING, NOTHING.

Louis Aragon, 'Dada Manifesto', 1920

For onely in destroying I find ease
To my relentless thoughts . . .
To mee shall be the glorie sole among
Th' infernal Powers, in one day to have marrd
What he *Almightie* styl'd, six Nights and Days
Continu'd making, and who knows how long
Before had bin contriving.

John Milton, *Paradise Lost*, IX, 129, 1667

We intend to sing the love of danger, the habit of energy and fearlessness.

Courage, audacity, and revolt will be the essential elements of our poetry. . . .

We say that the world's magnificence has been enriched by a new beauty; the beauty of speed. A racing car whose hood is adorned with great pipes, like serpents of explosive breath – a roaring car that seems to ride on grapeshot – is more beautiful than the 'Victory of Samothrace'.

We shall sing a hymn to the man at the wheel, who hurls the lance of his spirit across the Earth, along the circle of its orbit. . . .

We will glorify war – the world's only hygiene – militarism, patriotism, the destructive gesture of freedom-bringers, beautiful ideas worth dying for, and scorn for woman.

We will destroy the museums, libraries, academies of every kind, will fight moralism, feminism, every opportunistic or utilitarian cowardice.

We will sing of great crowds excited by work, by pleasure and by riot; we will sing of the multicolored, polyphonic tides of revolution in the modern capitals; we will sing of the vibrant nightly fervor of arsenals and shipyards blazing with violent electric moons; greedy railway stations that devour smoke-plumed serpents; factories hung on clouds by the crooked lines of their smoke; bridges that stride the rivers like giant gymnasts, flashing in the sun with a glitter of knives; adventurous steamers that sniff the horizon; deep-chested locomotives whose wheels paw the tracks like the hooves of enormous steel horses bridled by tubing; and the sleek flight of planes whose propellers chatter in the wind like banners and seem to cheer like an enthusiastic crowd.

F. T. Marinetti, 'Manifesto of Futurism', 1909

This new type of man . . . turns his interest away from life, persons, nature, ideas – in short from everything that is alive; he transforms all life into things, including himself and the manifestations of his human faculties of reasoning, seeing, hearing, tasting, loving. Sexuality becomes a technical skill . . . feelings are flattened and sometimes substituted for by sentimentality; joy, the expression of intense aliveness, is replaced by 'fun' or excitement; and whatever love and tenderness man has is directed toward machines and gadgets. The world becomes a sum of lifeless artefacts; from synthetic food to synthetic organs, the whole man becomes part of the total machinery that he controls and is simultaneously controlled by. He has no plan, no goal for life, except doing what the logic of technique determines him to do. He aspires to make robots as one of the greatest achievements of his technical mind, and some specialists assure us that the robot will hardly be distinguished from living men. This achievement will not seem so astonishing when man himself is hardly distinguishable from a robot.

The world of life has become a world of 'no-life'; persons have become 'nonpersons', a world of death.

Erich Fromm, *The Anatomy of Human Destructiveness*, 1974

In his hands the submachine gun is excited,
pouring its life out; he is detached,
searching for bodies. I am detached,
wondering whether to stuff and hang him
on my wall a trophy. From behind,
I could put a bullet through his head
and as he sinks dropping his gun,
rip off his clothes, slice him down the middle,
pull out his liver, heart, spleen,
the whole works from head to bowels,
his brain poked out through his nostrils
to keep his skull intact.
I'd leave his eyes in,
treat them chemically to last
for their lustrous quality.
I'd stuff with dried grass the cavities of his body
to achieve their natural proportions,
then glue him to the surface of a board
the length of his frame, hang him on the wall
in my study, the submachine gun stuck back
in his hands, his mouth straightened
in a killer's line, except
I lack his calculating way to do it,
and can only write this to say
in any case
he is finished.

David Ignatow, 'Soldier', 1968

Clouds of smoke darkened the sky; dive bombers tilted
and hurtled toward their goal; we could watch the flight of
the released bombs, the pull-out of the planes and the
cloud from the explosions expanding gigantically. The
effect was enhanced by running the film in slow motion.

Hitler was fascinated. The film ended with a montage showing a plane diving toward the outlines of the British Isles. A burst of flames followed, and the island flew into the air in tatters. Hitler's enthusiasm was unbounded. 'That is what will happen to them!' he cried out, carried away. 'That is how we will annihilate them!'

Albert Speer, on Hitler's reaction to the final scene of a newsreel about the bombing of Warsaw, 1970

The most cursory study of dream-life and of the phantasies of the insane shows that ideas of world-destruction (more accurately destruction of what the world symbolizes) are latent in the unconscious mind. And since the atomic bomb is less a weapon of war than a weapon of extermination it is well adapted to the more blood-thirsty phantasies with which man is secretly preoccupied during phases of acute frustration. Nagasaki destroyed by the magic of science is the nearest man has yet approached in the realization of dreams that even during the safe immobility of sleep are accustomed to develop into nightmares of anxiety. The first promise of the atomic age is that it can make some of our nightmares come true. The capacity so painfully acquired by normal men to distinguish between sleep, delusion, hallucination and the objective reality of waking life has for the first time in history been seriously weakened.

Edward Glover, *War, Sadism and Pacifism*, 1946

We were founded on a Declaration, on the Constitution, on principles, and we've always had the ideal of 'saving the world'. And that comes close to perhaps destroying the world. . . . We might blow up Cuba to save ourselves and then the whole world would blow up. Yet it would come in the guise of an idealistic stroke . . . yes, I suppose this is too apocalyptic to put it this way, but it is the Ahab story of having to murder evil: and then you may murder all the good with it if it gets desperate enough to struggle.

Robert Lowell, interview, 1965

And Samson said unto the lad that held him by the hand, Suffer me that I may feel the pillars whereupon the house standeth, that I may lean upon them. Now the house was full of men and women; and all the lords of the Philistines were there; and there were upon the roof about three thousand men and women. . . . And Samson took hold of the two middle pillars upon which the house stood, and on which it was borne up, of the one with his right hand, and of the other with his left. And Samson said, Let me die with the Philistines. And he bowed himself with all his might, and the house fell upon the lords, and upon all the people that were therein.

Judges 16: 26–30

Even if we are destroyed, England will at least lose India.

Kaiser Wilhelm, 1914

The only deterrent we can present to the Kremlin is evidence we give that we may make any of the critical points [in the world] which we cannot hold the occasion for a global war of annihilation.

US National Security Council document, NSC-68, 1950

❦

Nuclear weapons alter and blur the boundaries of our psychological lives, of our symbolic space, in ways crucial to our thought, feelings and actions. The most extreme state of contemporary deformation is a pattern which may best be called 'nuclearism'. By this term I mean to suggest the passionate embrace of nuclear weapons as a solution to our anxieties (especially our anxieties concerning the weapons themselves). That is, one turns to the weapons, and to their power, as means of restoring boundaries. Nuclearism, then, is a secular religion, a total ideology in which grace, mastery of death, is achieved by means of a new technological deity. This deity is seen as an all-powerful force, capable of both apocalyptic destruction and unlimited creation, and the nuclear believer, or nuclearist, allies himself to that force and feels compelled to expound the virtues of his god.

Robert Jay Lifton, *Boundaries*, 1969

❦

Some people used to claim that A-bombs, numbered in the thousands or tens of thousands, were beyond our reach. I am here to report to the Senate and the American people that the atomic bottlenecks are being broken. There is virtually no limit and no limiting factor upon the number of A-bombs which the United States can manufacture, given time and given a decision to proceed all out. . . .

We must have atomic weapons to use in the heights of

the sky and the depths of the sea; we must have them to use above the ground, on the ground, and below the ground. An aggressor must know that if he dares attack he will have no place to hide. . . .

Mark me well: massive atomic deterring power can win us years of grace, years in which to wrench history from its present course and direct it toward the enshrinement of human brotherhood.

Senator Brien M. McMahon, Speech to the US Senate,
18 September 1951

The effects could well be called unprecedented, magnificent, beautiful, stupendous and terrifying. No man-made phenomenon of such tremendous power had ever occurred before. The lighting effects beggared description. The whole country was lighted by a searing light with the intensity many times that of the midday sun. It was golden, purple, violet, gray and blue. It lighted every peak, crevasse and mountain range with a clarity and beauty that cannot be described but must be seen to be imagined. It was the beauty the great poets dream about but describe most poorly and inadequately. Thirty seconds after the explosion came, first the air blast pressing hard against people and things, to be followed almost immediately by the strong, sustained awesome roar which warned of doomsday and made us feel that we puny things were blasphemous to dare tamper with the forces heretofore reserved to The Almighty. Words are inadequate tools for the job of acquainting those not present with the physical, mental and psychological effects. It had to be witnessed to be realized.

Brigadier General Thomas Farrell, Official Report on the
first atom bomb test at Alamogordo, 16 July 1945

Writing on lined sheets of a legal-sized tablet in a bold but clear scrawl, Truman observed on July 15, 1945; 'We have discovered the most terrible weapon in the history of the world. It may be the fire destruction prophesied in the Euphrates Valley era, after Noah and his fabulous ark.'

The Times, 3 June 1980

❧⊙❧

World events in fulfilment of prophecy show that we are deep into the 'last days', in 'critical times hard to deal with' (2 Timothy 3: 1–5). This means that we are nearing the Biblical 'Armageddon' (Revelation 16:16). The magazine *Family Weekly* noted that many 'believe that the social order is collapsing, with Armageddon just around the corner'.

However, the approach of Armageddon should not be a cause for fear, but for real hope! Why? Because Armageddon is God's war to cleanse the earth of all wickedness, paving the way for a bright, prosperous new order! The Bible explains that the righteous 'will possess the earth, and they will indeed find their exquisite delight in the abundance of peace' (Psalm 37:11).

With bad conditions forever gone, every day of life then will be a delight. Not even sickness or death will mar the happiness of the people. God will 'wipe out every tear from their eyes, and death will be no more, neither will mourning nor outcry nor pain be nay more' (Revelation 21:4).

Circular from Jehovah's Witnesses, 1982

❧⊙❧

'I do not know how many future generations we can count on before the Lord returns.' – James Watt, US Secretary of State for the Interior★

'Jerry, I sometimes believe we're heading very fast for Armageddon right now.' – President Reagan★

'I have read the Book of Revelation and, yes, I believe the world is going to end – by an act of God, I hope – but every day I think that time is running out. . . . I think of World War II and how long it took to prepare for it, to convince people that rearmament for war is needed. I fear we will not be ready. I think time is running out . . . but I have faith.' – Caspar Weinberger, US Secretary of Defense†

★ Quoted in James L. Franklin, 'The Religious Right and the New Apocalypse', *Boston Globe*, 2 May 1982
† Interview, *New York Times*, 23 August 1982

Become an End-Time Partner by sending a generous contribution towards the launching of this End-Time Prophetic Ministry.
– I would like to participate in the World End-Time Ministry.
– I would like to receive your book, *The Antichrist Report*, when it's off the press.
– I would like to receive the *Prophetic Messenger*.
All contributions are deductible on the donor's income tax return.
THE END IS NEAR.

Circular distributed in the United States, 1983

No more ashes, no more sackcloth
And an armband made of black cloth
Will some day never more adorn a sleeve.
For if the bomb that drops on you
Gets your friends and neighbors too,
There'll be nobody left behind to grieve.

And we will all go together when we go,
What a comforting fact that is to know.
Universal bereavement,
An inspiring achievement,
Yes, we all will go together when we go.

Tom Lehrer, 'We Will All Go Together When We Go',
1959

. . . and, lo, there was a great earthquake; and the sun became black as sackcloth of hair, and the moon became as blood; And the stars of heaven fell unto the earth, even as a fig tree casteth her untimely figs, when she is shaken of a mighty wind. And the heaven departed as a scroll when it is rolled together; and every mountain and island were moved out of their places. And the kings of the earth, and the great men, and the rich men, and the chief captains, and the mighty men, and every bondman, and every free man, hid themselves in the dens and in the rocks of the mountains; And said to the mountains and rocks, Fall on us, and hide us from the face of him that sitteth on the throne, and from the wrath of the Lamb.

Revelation 6:12–16

it would be so exciting
it would be so powerful
it would punish us for our sins
things wouldn't be so boring anymore
we could get back to basics
we could remember who we love
it would be so loud
it would be so hot
the mushroom clouds would rise up
we could start over
we wouldn't have to be afraid of it anymore
we wouldn't have to be afraid anymore
we would finally have done it
   better than Raskolnikov
it would release our anger
   in the ultimate tantrum
then we could rest

Alia Johnson, 'Why We Should Drop the Bombs', 1981

'Do it beautifully!', says Hedda Gabler to Lovborg, as she hands him the gun. Oh yes, we'll do it beautifully. What more beautiful way to do it than in the way that poets dream about, but describe most poorly and inadequately? But the gun goes off by accident, and Lovborg dies miserably, shot not through the heart but through the balls.

Nicholas Humphrey, 'Four Minutes to Midnight', 1981

5

Nothing, but Who Knows Nothing

Alas, poor country!
Almost afraid to know itself! It cannot
Be called our mother but our grave, where nothing,
But who knows nothing, is once seen to smile;
Where sighs and groans, and shrieks that rend the air,
Are made, not marked; where violent sorrow seems
A modern ecstasy. The dead man's knell
Is there scarce asked for who; and good men's lives
Expire before the flowers in their caps,
Dying or ere they sicken.

William Shakespeare, *Macbeth*, IV, iii, 1606

The atomic bomb is a paper tiger which the US reactionaries use to scare people. It looks terrible, but in fact it isn't.

Mao Tse-tung, 1960

How will posterity believe that there has been a time when without the lightnings of heaven or the fires of earth, without wars or other visible slaughter, not this or that part of the earth, but well-nigh the whole globe, has remained without inhabitants?

When has any such thing been heard or seen; in what annals has it ever been read that houses were left vacant, cities deserted, the country neglected, the fields too small for the dead, and a fearful and universal solitude over the whole earth? Consult your historians, they are silent; question your doctors, they are dumb; seek an answer from your philosophers, they shrug their shoulders and frown, and with their fingers to their lips bid you be silent.

Will posterity ever believe these things when we, who see, can scarcely credit them? We should think we were dreaming if we did not with our eyes, when we walk abroad, see the city in mourning with funerals, and returning to our home, find it empty, and thus know that what we lament is real.

Survivor of the plague, quoted by Francis Gasquet, *The Great Pestilence*, 1893

It grew darker and darker. The already loud rumblings grew louder, and now they seemed all around us. The gusts of wind increased to such a hurricane as no man had ever experienced before. . . . The darkness became intense. The vivid lightning, which almost blinded us, seemed everywhere. . . . None of us will ever be able to describe the noise, especially one great bang around noon, which is supposed to have been the loudest sound ever heard on earth. It shook the people out of their beds in Batavia, 90 miles away. . . . Not that we knew or hardly cared what it was. The whole heavens seemed a blaze of fire. . . .

For some days after the convulsion the Sunda Strait was almost impassable and the sea was thick with dust and pumice. . . . Landmarks had disappeared and the coastline was hardly the same, and new islands had appeared in the main channels, brought up by the upheaval of the sea floor. We sailed near the spot where the city of Anger once stood, with its 36,000 inhabitants. The shores on each side looked burnt and sterile. Java, known as the Garden of the East, looked more like the Sahara.

R. J. Dalby, description of the eruption of Krakatoa, *Journal*, 1883

Walking next day upon the fateful shore,
Among the slaughtered bodies of their men
Which the full-stomached sea had cast upon
The sands, it was my unhappy chance to light
Upon a face, whose favour when it lived,
My astonished mind informed me I had seen.
He lay in's armour, as if that had been
His coffin; and the weeping sea, like one
Whose milder temper doth lament the death
Of him whom in his rage he slew, runs up
The shore, embraces him, kisses his cheek,
Goes back again, and forces up the sands
To bury him, and every time it parts
Sheds tears upon him, till at last (as if
It could no longer endure to see the man
Whom it had slain, yet loth to leave him) with
A kind of unresolved unwilling pace,
Winding her waves one in another, like
A man that folds his arms or wrings his hands
For grief, ebbed from the body, and descends
As if it would sink down into the earth,
And hide itself for shame of such a deed.

Cyril Tourneur, *The Atheist's Tragedy*, II, i, 1611

The birds were the things we could see all the time. They were superb specimens of life . . . really quite exquisite . . . phenomenal creatures. Albatrosses will fly for days, skimming a few inches above the surface of the water. These birds have tremendously long wings and tails, and beaks that are as if fashioned for another purpose. You don't see what these birds are about from their design, they are just beautiful creatures. Watching them is a wonder. That is what I didn't expect. . . .

We were standing around waiting for this bomb to go off, which we had been told was a very small one, so no one was particularly upset. Even though I'd never seen one, I figured, well, these guys know what is going to happen. They know what the dangers are and we've been adequately briefed and we all have our radiation meters on . . . No worry. . . .

Anyway, we were standing around, and the countdown comes in over the radio. And we knew roughly where the designated ground zero would be and about how high.

And suddenly I could see all these birds, I could see the birds that I'd been watching for days before. They were now suddenly visible through the opaque visor of my helmet. And they were smoking. Their feathers were on fire. And they were doing cartwheels. And the light persisted for some time. It was instantaneously bright but wasn't instantaneous, because it stayed and it changed its composition slightly. Several seconds, it seemed like, long enough for me to see birds crash into the water. They were sizzling, smoking. They weren't vaporized, it's just that they were absorbing such intense radiation that they were being consumed by the heat. Their feathers were on fire. They were blinded. And so far there had been no shock, none of the blast damage we talk about when we discuss the effects of nuclear weapons. Instead there were just these smoking, twisting, hideously contorted birds crashing into things. And then I could see vapor rising from the inner lagoon as the surface of the water was heated by this intense flash.

US atom test observer, Christmas Island, quoted by Robert Scheer, *With Enough Shovels*, 1982

The appearance of people was . . . well, they all had skin blackened by burns. They had no hair because their hair was burned, and at a glance you couldn't tell whether you were looking at them from in front or in back. They held their arms bent like this . . . and their skin – not only their hands, but on their faces and bodies too – hung down. If there had only been one or two such people perhaps I would not have had such a strong impression. But wherever I walked I met these people. Many of them died along the road – I can still picture them in my mind – like walking ghosts. They didn't look like people of this world. They had a special way of walking – very slowly. . . . I myself was one of them.

Hiroshima grocer, interviewed by Robert Jay Lifton, 1967

I climbed Hijiyama Hill and looked down. I saw that Hiroshima had disappeared. . . . I was shocked by the sight. . . . What I felt then and still feel now I just can't explain with words. Of course I saw many dreadful scenes after that – but that experience, looking down and finding nothing left of Hiroshima – was so shocking that I simply can't express what I felt. I could see Koi and a few buildings standing. . . . But Hiroshima didn't exist – that was mainly what I saw – Hiroshima just didn't exist.

Hiroshima history professor, interviewed by
Robert Jay Lifton, 1967

Those who were able walked silently towards the suburbs in the distant hills, their spirits broken, their initiative gone. When asked whence they had come, they pointed to

95

the city and said, 'that way'; and when asked where they were going, they pointed away from the city and said, 'this way'. They were so broken and confused that they moved and behaved like automatons.

Their reactions had astonished outsiders who reported with amazement the spectacle of long files of people holding stolidly to a narrow rough path when close by was a smooth, easy road going in the same direction. The outsiders could not grasp the fact that they were witnessing the exodus of a people who walked in the realm of dreams. . . . A spiritless people had forsaken a destroyed city.

M. Hachiya, *Hiroshima Diary*, 1955

❧◦❧

. . . the little spitting experimental bombs of Hiroshima and Nagasaki.

John Steinbeck, *Once There Was a War*, 1958

❧◦❧

Hiroshima and Nagasaki can provide us with no more than a hint of what would happen in the event of a nuclear war. A single weapon today can have the power of one thousand Hiroshima bombs, and we have to be able to imagine one thousand of these exploding in the space of a few minutes. Moreover, in the case of Hiroshima and Nagasaki – and this is absolutely crucial – there was still a functioning outside world to provide help. . . .

Imagine the familiar landscape turning suddenly into a sea of destruction. Everywhere smoldering banks of debris; everywhere the sights and sounds and smells of death. Imagine that the other survivors are wandering about with festering wounds, broken limbs, and bodies so badly burned that their features appear to be melting and their flesh peeling away in great raw folds. Imagine – on the generous assumption that your children are alive at all – that you have no way of knowing whether the radiation they have been exposed to has already doomed them.

The suddenness and the sheer ferocity of such a scene would not give the survivors any chance to mobilize the usual forms of psychological defense. The normal human response to mass death and profound horror is not rage or depression or panic or mourning or even fear; it is a kind of mental anesthetization that interferes with both judgment and compassion for other people.

In even minor disasters, the mind becomes immobilized, if only for a moment. But in the event of a nuclear attack, the immobilization may reach the point where the psyche is no longer connected to its own past and is, for all practical purposes, severed from the social forms from which it drew strength and a sense of humanity. The mind would, then, be shut down altogether.

The resulting scene might very well resemble what we usually can only imagine as science fiction. The landscape is almost moonlike, spare and quiet, and the survivors who root among the ruins seem to have lost contact with one another, not to mention the ability to form cooperating groups and to offer warmth and solace to people around them.

In every catastrophe for which we have adequate records, survivors emerge from the debris with the feeling that they are 'naked and alone . . . in a terrifying wilderness of ruins'.

In most cases – and this, too, is well recorded in the literature of disaster – that sense of isolation quickly disappears with the realization that the rest of the world is still intact. The disaster, it turns out, is local, confined, bounded. Out there beyond the peripheries of the affected zone are other people – relatives, neighbors, countrymen – who bring blankets and warm coffee, medicines and ambulances. The larger human community is gathering its resources to attend to a wound on its flank, and the survivors respond to the attention and the caring with the reassuring feeling that there is life beyond the ruins, after all. That sense of communion, that perception that the textures of social existence remain more or less whole, is a very important part of the healing that follows.

None of that will happen in nuclear war.

There will be no surrounding human community, no undamaged world out there to count on. . . .

The question so often asked, 'Would the survivors envy the dead?' may turn out to have a simple answer. No, they would be incapable of such feelings. They would not so much envy as, inwardly and outwardly, resemble the dead.

Robert Jay Lifton and Kai Erikson, *Nuclear War's Effect on the Mind,* 1982

❧⊙❧

My brother and sisters didn't get to the shelter in time, so they were burnt and crying. Half an hour later, my mother appeared. She was covered with blood. She had been making lunch at home when the bomb was dropped. . . .

My younger sisters died the next day. My mother – she also died the next day. And then my older brother died. . . .

The survivors made a pile of wood on the playground and began to cremate the corpses. My brother was burned. Mother also was burned and quickly turned to white bones which dropped down among the live coals. I cried as I looked on the scene. Grandmother was also watching, praying with a rosary. . . .

I am now in the fourth grade of Yamazato Primary School. The playground of terrible memories is now completely cleared and many friends play there happily. I play with my friends there too, but sometimes I suddenly remember that awful day. When I do, I squat down on the spot where we cremated our mother and touch the earth with my fingers. When I dig deep in the ground with a piece of bamboo, several pieces of charcoal appear. Looking at the spot for a while, I can dimly see my mother's image in the earth. So when I see someone else walking on that place, it makes me very angry.

> Fujio Tsujimoto, 5 years old when the atom bomb,
> 'Fat Man', was dropped on Nagasaki

> What happened – really happened
> What happened – really happened
> What happened – really happened
> I believe with perfect faith
> That I will have the strength to believe that
> What happened – really happened.

> T. Carmi, 'Anatomy of a War', 1977

6

There's a Nuclear War Going on Inside Me

'I don't know, I feel there's a nuclear war going on inside
me. It's terrible.'

Girl, aged 11, Brookline, Massachusetts, 1982

Some time ago a crazy dream came to me
I dreamt I was walkin' into World War Three.
I went to the doctor the very next day
To see what kinda words he could say.
He said it was a bad dream.
I wouldn't worry 'bout it none, though,
They were my own dreams and they're only in my head.

I said, 'Hold it, Doc, a World War passed through my
                                                    brain.'
He said, 'Nurse, get your pad, this boy's insane.'
He grabbed my arm, I said, 'Ouch!'
As I landed on the psychiatric couch,
He said, 'Tell me about it.'

Well, the whole thing started at 3 o'clock fast,
It was all over by quarter past.
I was down in the sewer with some little lover
When I peeked out from under the manhole cover
Wondering who turned the lights on. . . .

Well, I rung the fallout shelter bell
And I leaned my head and gave a yell,
'Give me a string bean, I'm a hungry man.'
A shotgun fired and away I ran.
I don't blame them too much though,
I know I look funny.

Well, I spied a girl and before she could leave,
'Let's go and play Adam and Eve.'
I took her by the hand and my heart it was thumpin'
When she said, 'Hey man, you crazy or sumpin',
You see what happened last time they started.'

Well, I seen a Cadillac window uptown
And there was nobody aroun'.
I got into the driver's seat
And I drove down 42nd Street
In my Cadillac.
Good car to drive after a war. . . .

I was feelin' kinda lonesome and blue,
I needed somebody to talk to.
So I called up the operator of time
Just to hear a voice of some kind.
'When you hear the beep
It will be three o'clock.'
She said that for over an hour
And I hung up.

Well, the doctor interrupted me just about then,
Sayin', 'Hey I've been havin' the same old dreams,
But mine was a little different you see.
I dreamt that the only person left after the war was me.
I didn't see you around.'

Well, now time passed and now it seems
Everybody's having them dreams. . . .

Bob Dylan, 'Talkin' World War III Blues', 1972

I am sending this cheque on behalf of my son John who took his own life. . . . I know it isn't much but I'll continue to send what people send to me in his memory. John has been terrified by the idea of nuclear war for most of his 23 years. . . . He is a poet and musician and much of his writing and composition dealt with the insanity of everyone around with regard to this horror. One of the things found on him when he was found hanging in his room was a clipping from the paper about the effects of potential nuclear war. John had many things on his mind but I can't help but wonder how badly we are hurting our young. He could no longer face it. The many who remain deserve better than what this crazy world is offering.

Letter to International Physicians for the Prevention of
Nuclear War, 1982

❖⊃∘⊂❖

Even if the worst does not happen, at least until our present children are grown up, we must still take into account the effect of living one's most formative years under the 'protection' of the nuclear deterrent. If attacked, we shall devastate our enemies' homeland in return; that is what the word deterrent implies. If, on the other hand, we make the first strike – and the United States has said that in a position of danger this may happen – we shall initiate the savagery ourselves.

What may our children learn from this? They learn that a community may call itself civilized and yet possess weapons which would once have been regarded as barbarous beyond belief. The middle-aged and old can perhaps preserve their innate sense of what it means to be civilized, having been brought up at a time when an attack on a field ambulance or an unarmed village provoked feelings of indignation. How will it be for our children, brought up to regard the infliction of widespread devastation on civilians as something we, in certain circumstances, may be forced to do? Surely, in deploying such weapons, we erode the moral base of what we are out to defend.

On several occasions I have sat in on discussion lessons when school children have brought up the question of the Bomb. Many have come to accept they may not live out their lives in full; they have also learned (from their elders) that nothing can be done. Some, quite literally, smile about it. Perhaps they confuse violence and death with its image on television, which does not hurt and can even be enjoyed. Others are most painfully aware of what is involved.

I remember one girl in particular who described how she tried to talk it over with her parents. They told her: 'It's no good worrying about it. There's nothing we can do. We'll face the problem when we have to.'

What difference would or could it make if our politicians were as painfully aware of the danger as that girl . . . ?

Philip Payne, County Inspector of Schools,
letter to *The Times*, 1981

> 'Father, father, where are you going?
> O do not walk so fast.
> Speak father, speak to your little boy,
> Or else I shall be lost.'
>
> The night was dark, no father was there;
> The child was wet with dew;
> The mire was deep, and the child did weep,
> And away the vapour flew.

William Blake, 'The Little Boy Lost', 1789

'There is a film that tells how a war almost broke out between America and the Soviet Union, and after that I didn't sleep for several nights thinking about this, about how war almost broke out and how our existence is hanging on a thread.' – Oleg, aged 15, from the Ukraine

'When I watch films or listen to the radio, I can imagine immediately how bombs will fall on my village. And sometimes at night, I cover myself with the blankets, because I'm afraid.' – Sveta, aged 11, from Georgievskoye

'If war starts, we might all be without parents.' – Oskana, aged 11, from Moscow.

> Eric Chivian, John E. Mack and Jeremy Waletzky,
> interviews with Soviet children, 1983

'I just kept thinking about having to get killed by nuclear bombs, and sometimes I didn't want to go to sleep 'cause I was afraid I was going to have a really bad dream about a nuclear war and get killed or something. Maybe my parents and my friends and all my family would get killed and I'd just be alive and I wouldn't know what to do or anything. And I'd just be stuck.' – Boy, aged 9

'I sometimes think that I'd rather be dead because then I could go up to heaven and I wouldn't have to worry about all this stuff about nuclear war.' – Girl, aged 9

'I think I'd rather live in BC where there were no people. Well, there were people, but there were no war kinds. And I think that, I always keep on thinking that when I grow up I'm going to be an astronaut but I think I'm never going to be one. War's going to keep going on and nuclear missiles are going to keep on bombing countries and stuff. I think I will be dead and I'll never survive.' – Boy, aged 9

'I tell my mom that I'm never going to have a child because if I do then I'll die and also my child will. And I'm not that scared about myself because I'm myself, I'm one person. But, like, you know, if everybody in the world got killed then there'd be nobody left.' Girl, aged 9

Eric Chivian and Roberta Snow, interviews with schoolchildren in Brookline, Massachusetts, 1982

But the children, I think, should not be blotted out,
as I sit listening to the rise and fall
of their pleasures, the sudden change
to bad temper quickly forgotten
by the shift to joy. . . .

David Ignatow, 'A Meditation on Violence', 1968

Many children are concerned about the threat of nuclear war and experience troubling feelings of fear, sadness, powerlessness and rage.

[This] worry has increased in the period 1975–1983, as the nuclear arms competition has appeared to become increasingly out of control.

[There is] a perception that authority for nuclear war has slipped out of human control and has been taken over by technology.

Children and adolescents seem less defended than adults and more able to perceive the reality of what nuclear weapons can do and what nuclear war would really mean for them, their families and the world.

Many children feel they have no one with whom they can discuss the nuclear problem. They feel alone with their fears and abandoned, isolated and unprotected by the adult generation, including their nation's leaders. This adds to the sense of hopelessness and creates cynicism.

[They] express uncertainty about whether there will be a future. This futurelessness has raised questions for a number of investigators about the possible impact of the nuclear threat on personality development in childhood and adolescence. There are no systematic data on this subject.

> John E. Mack, Professor of Psychiatry at Harvard University, testimony to Select Committee of the US House of Representatives, 1983

⋘∘⋙

To lose the future means to lose the past as well, to give up on history. It is to repress the sense of death and life alike, for both death and life can only be experienced as part of a continuum of existence. It is to retreat to the narrowest sliver of the present, and to guard one's interest there in a self-centred manner. Yet we do not succeed in living fully in the present either – because the only present in which we can live fully is a present into which all existence has been compressed. And so when we lose the future, we lose the present as well.

> Joel Kovel, *Against the State of Nuclear Terror*, 1983

⋘∘⋙

The fact that we die is one of the difficult lessons of early childhood. The capacity to learn that lesson, which we all succeed at only imperfectly, depends upon death having some appropriateness: the idea that one dies after a good deal of living; that old people die rather than young ones.

But now death becomes associated with massive, grotesque extermination that consumes the young, as well as the old, those who have not yet lived their lives, as well as

109

those who have. Inevitable individual death becomes confused with unacceptable meaningless annihilation.

Robert Jay Lifton, testimony to Select Committee of the
US House of Representatives, 1983

∗⋑∘⋐∗

I cannot listen to Mahler's Ninth Symphony with anything
like the old melancholy mixed with high pleasure I used to
take from this music. There was a time, not long ago,
when what I heard, especially in the final movement, was
an open acknowledgement of death and at the same time a
quiet celebration of the tranquillity connected to the process. I
took this music as a metaphor for reassurance, confirming
my own strong hunch that the dying of every living
creature, the most natural of all experiences, has to be a
peaceful experience. . . .

Now I hear it differently. I cannot listen to the last
movement of the Mahler Ninth without the door-smashing
intrusion of a huge new thought: death everywhere, the
dying of everything, the end of humanity. The easy sadness
expressed with such gentleness and delicacy by that repeated
phrase on faded strings, over and over again, no longer
comes to me as old, familiar news of the cycle of living and
dying. All through the last notes my mind swarms with
images of a world in which the thermonuclear bombs have
begun to explode, in New York and San Francisco,
in Moscow and Leningrad, in Paris, in Paris, in Paris.
In Oxford and Cambridge, in Edinburgh. I cannot push
away the thought of a cloud of radioactivity drifting
along the Engadin, from the Moloja Pass to Ftan, killing
off the part of the earth I love more than any other part.

I am old enough by this time to be used to the notion of
dying, saddened by the glimpse when it has occurred but
only transiently knocked down, able to regain my feet

quickly at the thought of continuity, any day. I have acquired and held in affection until very recently another sideline of an idea which serves me well at dark times: the life of the earth is the same as the life of an organism: the great round being possesses a mind: the mind contains an infinite number of thoughts and memories: when I reach my time I may find myself still hanging around in some sort of midair, one of those small thoughts, drawn back into the memory of the earth: in that peculiar sense I will be alive.

Now all that has changed. I cannot think that way anymore. Not while those things are still in place, aimed everywhere, ready for launching.

That is a bad enough thing for the people in my generation. We can put up with it, I suppose, since we must. We are moving along anyway, like it or not. I can even set aside my private fancy about hanging around in midair.

What I cannot imagine, what I cannot put up with, the thought that keeps grinding its way into my mind, making the Mahler into a hideous noise close to killing me, is what it must be like to be young. How do the young stand it? How can they keep their sanity? If I were very young, sixteen or seventeen years old, I think I would begin, perhaps very slowly and imperceptibly, to go crazy.

Lewis Thomas, *Late Night Thoughts on
Listening to Mahler's Ninth Symphony*, 1983

~✦~

Last November [1980] a Gallup poll revealed that 39% of British adults expect a nuclear war in their lifetime. During the previous May, a National Opinion Poll disclosed that 65% of us foresee a third world war during the same timespan.

Many of us manage to behave as if there might be a

111

future at the same time as saying there is none. We suffer graphic imaginings of a post-holocaust world, while simultaneously knowing it is unimaginable. Or we console ourselves with the thought that we'll all go up in a big flash and know nothing about it. Instant obliteration is not only contemplated, but hoped for . . . a measure of the dreadful shift in consciousness that has happened in the last year.

Apocalyptic war-talk manifests itself in millions of conversations. Since most of us are unclear as to what would be the series of events that lead to a nuclear attack, all sorts of external events take on a doom-laden quality. . . . Thousands of people think intolerable thoughts.

Ellen (not her real name, for she didn't want to admit her fears publicly), married with two young daughters, lives in Sheffield. In common with many others who live in that city, she believes that the local coalmining and steel industries put it in the front line for a nuclear attack. Ellen has frequent waking nightmares about what will happen. 'We are all cooped up in a tiny space, in the dark. It's freezing cold and there's nothing to eat. Everything outside is contaminated, people are screaming with grief, going berserk. We are injured, and the children are in total panic. I have to think about how to kill them, and myself, and how to do it painlessly. . . .'

Keren Abse, a teacher in a comprehensive school in North West London, told me about a recent school survey on attitudes to nuclear war. 'Everybody in my class thought we should have unilateral disarmament, and half of them thought that America will start a nuclear war.'

Keren has found it hard to deal with the frequent classroom panics and questions about war, since the children want her to give reassurance about something in which she has little hope. Steve Bailey, who teaches in Walworth, agrees. 'We have the same fears as the children, but because we are adults and teachers they see us as representatives of the status quo, and of the government. They want us to pacify them, to dismiss fears, and say "no there isn't going to be a war, don't worry about it, get on with your writing."'

Steve says that teenagers who have been demoralized by lack of employment prospects are even less interested in working for exams. 'They say "we'll all be dead in ten years, so why bother?" There is just no answer to that.' For some children the fear is more immediate. One 13-year-old boy wept because 'there's going to be a war – my mummy's in America and she'll be dead'. Another miserably confessed that she 'can't commit suicide – I'm a Catholic'. Keren told me about two boys who were fantasizing about what they'd do in the event of a ten minute warning. 'It'd be great,' said one, 'I could go round and screw everybody.' The other joined in, 'Yeah . . . you could murder everyone!'

Rose Shapiro, 'Terrorism', *Time Out*, 6 February 1981

Last night I was dreaming,
Dreamed about the H-bomb. . . .
There were thirteen women,
And me the only man in town.

Bill Haley, 'Thirteen Women', 1956

Very Last Day; 'A' Bomb in Wardour Street; The End; Had Enough; Eve of Destruction; Judgement Day: A Hard Rain's Gonna Fall; On the Road to Kingdom Come; Time is Running Out; Waiting for the End of the World; I'm Scared.

The *Rock Music Source Book*, 1980, lists forty-three songs under the heading 'Apocalyptic: Songs that have to do with imminent disaster or total destruction'

Piping down the valleys wild,
Piping songs of pleasant glee,
On a cloud I saw a child,
And he laughing said to me:

'Pipe a song about a Lamb!'
So I piped with merry chear.
Piper, pipe that song again;'
So I piped; he wept to hear.

'Drop thy pipe, thy happy pipe,
Sing thy songs of happy chear.'
So I sung the same again
While he wept with joy to hear.

William Blake, 'Introduction', *Songs of Innocence*, 1789

Tell us, doctors of philosophy, what are the needs of a
man. At least a man needs to be . . . notafraid nothungry
notcold not without love.

John Dos Passos, *The Big Money*, 1936

7

Hope Abandoned

Perhaps in determinism complete lies the perfect peace I have so longed for. Free-will, I've tried, and rejected it.

T. E. Lawrence, letter

We have become passive, fascinated spectators of the slowly unfolding nuclear Tragedy. I was taught at school that the essential quality of a tragic play is this: when the curtain rises you see a gun on the wall, and you know that in the last act the hero or heroine will take the gun from the wall and shoot themselves. It has to be so, the internal logic of the play allows no other ending. . . .

It is easy for those of us who are not historians to kid ourselves that nothing like this has ever happened before – and that because it has never happened before, it cannot really be happening now. But it *has* happened before, if never on such a disastrous scale. There are in fact dreadful precedents in history: times when whole groups of human beings, men and women whose love of life was no less than our own, have gone almost without protest to destruction. I think of the long-suffering European Jews in the last war . . . of the way those numbed souls patiently took the trains to the extermination camps . . . of what happened in 1942 in the ravine near Kiev known as Babi Yar, where thousand upon thousand queued up for execution, mothers and fathers hand in hand with children, shuffling their way slowly forward till they reached the front of the line and were gunned down. I think of the victims of the Stalinist purges in the Russia of the 1930s . . . of the way, week by week, people saw their comrades disappear into the torture chambers and the jails, they knew they would be next – and waited. . . .

Psychologists recognize two kinds of helplessness. *Learned* helplessness may develop when, for example, a person has repeatedly found that previous efforts to take control of his own life have genuinely come to nothing; he loses all faith in his own effectiveness and carries over to the present a picture of himself as someone unable any longer to influence events.

But there is also a different sort of helplessness: a *superstitious* helplessness where a person's belief in his own impotence has no basis in experience, but results instead from nothing more than a superstitious premonition that his life, and perhaps the life of the whole world, is set on an unalterable course – unalterable, that is, by human agency. The belief, for example, that his own fate has been sealed by a specific curse; or that, the world over, God and the Devil are working out their higher purposes without care for individual human beings. 'No more' than such a superstitious premonition – but superstitious helplessness can take the fight out of a man quite as effectively as any more reasonable fear. Cordelia Edvardson, one of the delegates to the 1981 reunion of Holocaust survivors, described how some of the Jews in Germany fell victim to just such a paralysing superstition: 'Of course,' she says, 'we wanted to survive, but we were not at all sure we had the right to survive.' And when a person no longer believes he has the right to survive, his helplessness itself is killing. . . .

We behave at times as though we have been hexed by the Bomb, put under a spell.

Nicholas Humphrey, 'Four Minutes to Midnight', 1981

The spring is wound up tight. It will uncoil of itself. The least little turn of the wrist will do the job. Anything will set it going: a glance at a girl who happens to be lifting her arms to her hair as you go by; a feeling when you wake up on a fine morning that you'd like a little respect paid to you today, as if it were as easy to order as a second cup of coffee; one question too many, idly thrown out over a friendly drink – and the tragedy is on.

The rest is automatic. You don't need to lift a finger. The machine is in perfect order, it has been oiled ever since time began, and it runs without friction. Death, treason and sorrow are on the march; and they move in the wake of storm, of tears, of stillness. . . .

Tragedy is clean, it is restful, it is flawless. . . . In a tragedy, nothing is in doubt and everyone's destiny is known. That makes for tranquillity. There is a sort of fellow-feeling among characters in a tragedy: he who kills is as innocent as he who gets killed: it's all a matter of what part you are playing. Tragedy is restful; and the reason is that hope, that foul, deceitful thing, has no part in it. There isn't any hope. You're trapped.

Jean Anouilh, *Antigone*, 1942

◈〜◦〜◈

The coach gradually filled with other passengers. The door to our compartment was guarded by a soldier who turned back passengers eager to find places – the rest of the coach was crammed. M. [Osip Mandelstam] stayed by the window, desperate for contact with the two men on the other side, but no sound could penetrate the glass. Our ears were powerless to hear, and the meaning of their gestures hard to interpret. A barrier had been raised between us and the world outside. It was still a transparent one, made of glass, but it was already impenetrable. The train started for Sverdlosk.

At the moment I entered the coach and saw our brothers through the glass, my world split into two halves. Everything that had previously existed now vanished to become a dim memory, something beyond the looking-glass, and the future no longer meshed with the past. I am not trying to be literary – this is just a modest attempt to put into words the mental dislocation that is probably felt by all the many people who cross this fateful line. Its first result was utter indifference to what we had left behind. . . .

Until a short time before, I had been full of concern for all my friends and relatives, for my work, for everything I set store by. Now this concern was gone – and fear, too. Instead there was an acute sense of being doomed – it was this that gave rise to an indifference so overwhelming as to be almost physical, like a heavy weight pressing down on the shoulders. I also felt that time, as such, had come to an end – there was only an interlude before the inescapable swallowed us with our 'Europe' and our handful of last thoughts and feelings.

How would it come, the inescapable? Where, and in what form? It really didn't matter. Resistance was useless. Having entered a realm of non-being, I had lost the sense of death. In the face of doom, even fear disappears. Fear is a gleam of hope, the will to live, self-assertion. It is a deeply European feeling, nurtured on self-respect, the sense of one's own worth, rights, needs and desires. A man clings to what is his, and fears to lose it. Fear and hope are bound up with each other. Losing hope, we lose fear as well – there is nothing to be afraid for.

When a bull is being led to the slaughter, it still hopes to break loose and trample its butchers. Other bulls have not been able to pass on the knowledge that this never happens and that from the slaughterhouse there is no way back to the herd. But in human society there is a continuous exchange of experience. I have never heard of a man who broke away and fled while being led to his execution. It is even thought to be a special form of courage if a man about to be executed refuses to be blindfolded and dies with his eyes open. But I would rather have the bull with his blind rage, the stubborn beast who doesn't weigh his chances of survival with the prudent dull-wittedness of man, and doesn't know the despicable feeling of despair.

Later I often wondered whether it is right to scream when you are being beaten and trampled underfoot. Isn't it better to face one's tormentors in a stance of satanic pride, answering them with contemptuous silence? I decided that it is better to scream. This pitiful sound, which sometimes, goodness knows how, reaches into the remotest prison cell, is a concentrated expression of the last vestige of human dignity. It is a man's way of leaving a trace, of telling people how he lived and died. By his screams he asserts his right to live, sends a message to the outside world demanding help and calling for resistance. If nothing else is left, one must scream. Silence is the real crime against humanity.

That evening, guarded by three soldiers in the coach to which I had been taken in such comfort, I had lost everything, even despair. There is a moment of truth when you are overcome by sheer astonishment: 'So that's where I'm living, and the sort of people I'm living with! So this is what they're capable of! So this is the world I live in!' We are so stupefied that we even lose the power to scream. It was this sort of stupefaction, with the consequent loss of all criteria, standards and values, that came over people when they first landed in prison and suddenly realized the nature of the world they lived in and what the 'new era' really meant. Physical torture and fear are not enough to explain the way people broke down and confessed, destroying others in the process. All this was only possible at the 'moment of truth', during the madness which afflicted people when it looked as though time had stopped, the world had come to an end and everything was lost for ever. The collapse of all familiar notions is, after all, the end of the world.

Nadezhda Mandelstam, *Hope Against Hope*, 1971

One lioness and a young bull [buffalo] battled off and on for an hour and a half, the buffalo whirling round to face the cat with lowered horns whenever she came close, until finally she gave up and permitted him to walk away, only some scratches on the rump and a severed tail as remembrance of his encounter. But on another occasion five males came across an old bull. He stood in a swamp, belly deep in mud and water, safely facing his tormentors on the shore. Suddenly, inexplicably, he plodded toward them, intent it seemed on committing suicide. One lion grabbed his rump, another placed his paws on the bull's back and bit into the hump. Slowly, without trying to defend himself, the buffalo sank to his knees. There were no violent actions, no frantic movements, as the buffalo rolled onto his back and, with one lion holding his throat and another his muzzle, died of suffocation.

George Schaller, *Serengeti: Kingdom of Predators*, 1973

I remember a girl, slim and with black hair, who passed close to me, pointed to herself, and said 'Twenty-three.' . . . The people, completely naked, went down some steps which were cut in the clay wall of the pit and clambered over the heads of the people lying there, to the place where the SS man directed them. Then they lay down in front of the dead or injured people; some caressed those who were still alive and spoke to them in a low voice. Then I heard a series of shots.

Eyewitness report of Nazi execution, quoted by Raul Hilberg, *The Destruction of European Jews*, 1961

A Brazilian Indian condemned and sentenced by a medicine man, is helpless against his own emotional response to this pronouncement – and dies within hours. . . . In New Zealand a Maori woman eats fruit that she only later learns has come from a tabooed place. Her chief has been profaned. By noon of the next day she is dead. In Australia a witch doctor points a bone at a man. Believing that nothing can save him, the man rapidly sinks in spirits and prepares to die.

Walter Cannon, 'Voodoo Death', 1942

⋙⃝⋘

When, in early 1973, medical officer Major F. Harold Kushner returned from five and a half years as a prisoner of war in South Vietnam, he told me a stark and chilling tale. His story represents one of the few cases on record in which a trained medical observer witnessed from start to finish what I can only call death from helplessness. . . .

When Major Kushner arrived at First Camp in January 1968, Robert had already been captive for two years. He was a rugged and intelligent corporal from a crack marine unit, austere, stoic, and oblivious to pain and suffering. He was 24 years old and had been trained as a parachutist and scuba diver. Like the rest of the men, he was down to a weight of ninety pounds . . .[but] he remained in very good physical and mental health. The cause of his relatively fine shape was clear to Kushner. Robert was convinced that he would soon be released. The Viet Cong had made it a practice to release, as examples, a few men who had cooperated with them and adopted the correct attitudes. Robert had done so. . . . He made the statements required and was told to expect release within the month.

The month came and went. . . . It dawned on him that he had been deceived – that he had already served his

123

captor's purpose, and he wasn't going to be released. He stopped working and showed signs of severe depression: he refused food and lay on his bed in a fetal position, sucking his thumb. His fellow prisoners tried to bring him around. They hugged him, babied him, and when this didn't work, tried to bring him out of his stupor with their fists. . ... After a few weeks it was apparent to Kushner that Robert was moribund: although otherwise his gross physical shape was still better than most of the others, he was dusky and cyanotic. In the early hours of a November morning he lay dying in Kushner's arms. For the first time in days his eyes focused and he spoke: 'Doc, Post Office Box 161, Texarkana, Texas. Mom, Dad, I love you very much. Barbara, I forgive you.' Within seconds he was dead. . . .

Hope of release sustained Robert. When he gave up hope, when he believed that all his efforts had failed and would continue to fail, he died.

Can a psychological state be lethal? I believe it can.

Martin E. P. Seligman, *Helplessness*, 1975

⋙∘⋘

Each and everyone renounced all concern for life. The grapes, which are the principal wealth of the district, remained hanging on the vines and all prepared themselves for death. . . . They seemed to have resigned themselves as to a necessity and to regard it as a universal and inevitable doom. . . . One man, while still healthy, was digging his grave; some others lay down in theirs while they were yet alive and one of my labourers, as he was dying, shovelled the earth down over himself with his hands and feet.

Michel de Montaigne, Account of plague, *Essays*, 1585

⋙∘⋘

Victims of a nuclear strike in Bognor would be given burial at sea, the town's Neighbourhood Council was told. A guest speaker from Felpham Neighbourhood Council said: 'We are very lucky here because we are by the sea, so all the dead people can be taken out in a rowing boat, weighted down, and buried.'

Portsmouth Evening News, June 1983

There was an Old Man in a boat,
Who said, 'I'm afloat! I'm afloat!'
When they said, 'No! You ain't!' he was ready to faint,
That unhappy Old Man in a boat.

Edward Lear, *A Book of Nonsense*, 1846

Long before Orson Welles's broadcast had ended, people all over the United States were praying, crying, fleeing frantically to escape death from the Martians. Some ran to rescue loved ones. Others telephoned farewells and warnings, hurried to inform neighbors, sought information from newspapers or radio stations, summoned ambulances and police cars. . . .

[But] others adopted an attitude of complete resignation:

'I . . . kept on saying, what can we do, what difference does it make whether we die sooner or later? We were holding each other. Everything seemed unimportant in the face of death.' . . .

'I didn't do anything. I just kept listening. I thought if this is the real thing you only die once – why get excited? When the time comes you go and there is no getting away from it.' . . .

'My husband said we were here for God's glory and

125

honor and it was for Him to decide when we should die. We should prepare ourselves.'. . .

> Hadley Cantril, *The Invasion from Mars*, an account of reactions to the 'War of the Worlds', broadcast 30 October 1938

The continuing nuclear weapons cycle in any country depends on the collusion, or at least compliance, of most of the people. . . . But we can now identify a certain psychological combination taking shape: Fear and a sense of threat break through the prior stage of numbing; these uncomfortable feelings in turn raise the personal question of whether one should take some form of action to counter the danger; that question becomes an additional source of conflict, associated as it is with feelings of helplessness and doubts about efficacy; and one seeks a psychological safe haven of resignation ('Well, if it happens, it happens – and it will happen to all of us') and cynicism ('They'll drop it all right and it will be the end of all of us – that's the way people are, and that will be that'). That stance prevents one from feeling too fearful, and, equally important, it protects one from conflict and anxiety about doing something about the situation. If the situation is hopeless, one need do nothing. There is a particularly sophisticated version of resignation–cynicism that one encounters these days mainly at universities, which goes something like this: 'Well, what is so special about man? Other species have come and gone, so perhaps this is our turn to become extinct.' This is perhaps the ultimate above-the-battle position. Again nothing is to be done, one is philosophically – cosmically – detached from it all. All of these add up to a stance of *waiting for the bomb* and contribute to a self-fulfilling prophecy of universal doom.

> Robert Jay Lifton, *Indefensible Weapons*, 1982

Do not go gentle into that good night,
Old age should burn and rave at close of day;
Rage, rage against the dying of the light.

Though wise men at their end know dark is right,
Because their words had forked no lightning they
Do not go gentle into that good night.

Good men, the last wave by, crying how bright
Their frail deeds might have danced in a green bay,
Rage, rage against the dying of the light.

Wild men who caught and sang the sun in flight,
And learn, too late, they grieved it on its way,
Do not go gentle into that good night.

Grave men, near death, who see with blinding sight
Blind eyes could blaze like meteors and be gay,
Rage, rage against the dying of the light.

And you, my father, there on the sad height,
Curse, bless, me now with your fierce tears, I pray.
Do not go gentle into that good night.
Rage, rage against the dying of the light.

Dylan Thomas, 'Do not go gentle into that good night' 1952

It was a restless transport [at Auschwitz]. . . . Our Polish
Jews knew what was up. And so the whole place swarmed
with SS, and Schillinger, seeing what was going on, drew
his revolver. But everything would have gone smoothly
except that Schillinger had taken a fancy to a certain body
– and, indeed, she had a classic figure. That's what he had
come to see the chief about, I suppose. So he walked up to

the woman and took her by the hand. But the naked woman bent down suddenly, scooped up a handful of gravel and threw it in his face, and when Schillinger cried out in pain and dropped his revolver, the woman snatched it up and fired several shots into his abdomen. The whole place went wild. The naked crowd turned on us, screaming. The woman fired once again, this time at the chief. . . .

Schillinger was lying face down, clawing the dirt in pain with his fingers. We lifted him off the ground and carried him – not too gently – to a car. On the way he kept groaning through clenched teeth: '*O Gott, mein Gott, was hab' ich getan, dass ich so leiden muss*?', which means – O God, my God, what have I done to deserve such suffering?

Tadeusz Borowski, 'The Death of Schillinger', 1976

8

Different Drummers

If a man does not keep pace with his companions, perhaps it is because he hears a different drummer. Let him step to the music which he hears, however measured or far away.

Henry Thoreau, *Walden*, 1854

. . . . Finally he crawled down to the wall of the Country of the Blind and tried to make terms. He crawled along by the stream, shouting, until two blind men came out to the gate and talked to him.

He told them he was wiser now, and repented of all that he had done. . . .

He expected dire punishments, but these blind people were capable of toleration. They regarded his rebellion as but one more proof of his general idiocy and inferiority; and after they had whipped him they appointed him to do the simplest and heaviest work they had for any one to do, and he, seeing no other way of living, did submissively what he was told.

He was ill for some days, and they nursed him kindly. They refined his submission. But they insisted on his lying in the dark, and that was a great misery. And blind philosophers came and talked to him of the wicked levity of his mind. . . .

So Nunez became a citizen of the Country of the Blind, and these people ceased to be a generalized people and became individualities and familiar to him, while the world beyond the mountains became more and more remote and unreal. There was Yacob, his master, a kindly man when not annoyed; and there was Medina-sarote, who was the youngest daughter of Yacob.

. . . It was one of her eldest sisters who first told Yacob that Medina-sarote and Nunez were in love. . . . There was from the first very great opposition to the marriage. . . .

Old Yacob had a tenderness for his last little daughter, and was grieved to have her weep upon his shoulder.

'You see, my dear, he's an idiot. He has delusions; he can't do anything right.'

'I know,' wept Medina-sarote. 'But he's better than he was. He's getting better. . . . And he loves me – and father, I love him.'

Old Yacob was greatly distressed to find her inconsolable, and, besides – what made it more distressing – he liked Nunez for many things. So he went and sat in the window-less council-chamber with the other elders and watched the trend of the talk, and said, at the proper time, 'He's better than he was. Very likely, some day, we shall find him as sane as ourselves.'

Then afterwards one of the elders, who thought deeply, had an idea. . . .

'I have examined Nunez', he said, 'and the case is clear to me. I think very probably he might be cured.'

'That is what I have always hoped,' said old Yacob.

'His brain is affected,' said the blind doctor.

The elders murmured assent.

'Now *what* affects it?'

'*This,*' said the doctor, answering his own question. 'These queer things that are called the eyes . . . are diseased in such a way as to affect his brain. They are greatly distended, he has eyelashes, and his eyelids move, and consequently his brain is in a state of constant irritation and distraction.'

'Yes?' said old Yacob. 'Yes?'

'And I think I may say with reasonable certainty that, in order to cure him completely, all that we need do is a simple and easy surgical operation – namely, to remove these irritant bodies.'

'And then he will be sane?'

'Then he will be perfectly sane, and a quite admirable citizen.'

'Thank Heaven for science!' said old Yacob. . . .

For a week before the operation that was to raise him from his servitude and inferiority to the level of a blind citizen, Nunez knew nothing of sleep, and all through the warm sunlit hours, while the others slumbered happily, he sat brooding or wandered aimlessly. . . . At last work-time was over, the sun rose in splendour over the golden crests, and his last day of vision began for him. He had a few minutes with Medina-sarote before she went apart to sleep.

'Tomorrow,' he said, 'I shall see no more.'

'Dear heart!' she answered, and pressed his hands with all her strength. . . .

He held her in his arms, and pressed his lips to hers, and looked on her sweet face for the last time.

'Goodbye!' he whispered at that dear sight, 'goodbye!'

And then in silence he turned away from her.

He had fully meant to go to a lonely place where the meadows were beautiful with white narcissus, and there remain until the hour of his sacrifice should come, but as he went he lifted up his eyes and saw the morning, the morning like an angel in golden armour, marching down the steeps. . . .

He did not turn aside as he had meant to do, but went on, and passed through the wall of the circumference and out upon the rocks, and his eyes were always upon the sunlit ice and snow. . . . Then very circumspectly he began to climb. . . .

H. G. Wells, 'The Country of the Blind', 1904

And when we say that man is responsible for himself, we do not mean that he is responsible only for his own individuality, but that he is responsible for all men. . . .

When we say that man chooses himself, we do mean that every one of us must choose himself; but by that we also mean that in choosing for himself he chooses for all men. For in effect, of all the actions a man may take in order to create himself as he wills to be, there is not one which is not creative, at the same time, of an image of man such as he believes he ought to be. To choose between this or that is at the same time to affirm the value of that which is chosen; for we are unable ever to choose the worse. What we choose is always the better; and nothing can be better for us unless it is better for all. . . . Our responsibility is thus much greater than we had supposed, for it concerns mankind as a whole. . . . In fashioning myself I fashion man.

Jean-Paul Sartre, *Existentialism and Humanism*, 1946

These few words are being set down here as they come from my mind and my heart. And if I must write them with my hands in chains, I find that much better than if my will were in chains. . . .

For us men there are only two possibilities in this world: either we become ever better or ever worse; there is simply no such thing as standing still. Yes, even for those who have worked hard to come closer to God, there can be many reverses, just as an army advancing towards its victory does not win all its battles but must endure many defeats. Nevertheless, this does not mean that the struggle should be given up as hopeless; instead one must pick himself up with renewed strength and strive on again towards the desired goals. . . .

Many actually believe quite simply that things have to be the way they are. If this should happen to mean that they are obliged to commit injustice, then they believe that others are responsible. The oath would not be a lie for someone who believes he can go along and is willing to do so. But if I know in advance that I cannot accept and obey everything I would promise under that oath, then I would be guilty of a lie. For this reason I am convinced that it is still best that I speak the truth, even if it costs me my life. For you will not find it written in any of the commandments of God or of the Church, that a man is obliged under pain of sin to take an oath committing him to obey whatever might be commanded of him by his secular ruler. . . .

Dear wife, forgive me everything by which I have grieved or offended you. For my part, I have forgiven everything. Ask all those in Radegund whom I have ever injured or offended to forgive me too.

Franz Jagerstatter, last letter from prison, August 1943.
Jagerstatter, an Austrian farmer, was conscripted into
Hitler's army in February 1943, refused to take the
military oath of obedience and was beheaded
in Berlin on 9 August 1943

I shall die, but that is all that I shall do for Death.

I hear him leading his horse out of the stall; I hear the
   clatter on the barn-floor.
He is in haste; he has business in Cuba, business in the
   Balkans, many calls to make this morning.
But I will not hold the bridle while he cinches the
   girth.
And he may mount by himself; I will not give him a
   leg up.

Though he flick my shoulders with his whip, I will not
    tell him which way the fox ran.
With his hoof on my breast, I will not tell him where
    the black boy hides in the swamp.
I shall die, but that is all that I shall do for Death; I
    am not on his pay-roll.

I will not tell him the whereabouts of my friends nor
    of my enemies either.
Though he promise me much, I will not map him the
    route to any man's door.
Am I a spy in the land of the living, that I should
    deliver men to Death?
Brother, the password and the plans of our city are
    safe with me; never through me
Shall you be overcome.

Edna St Vincent Millay, 'Conscientious Objector', 1917

There are thousands who are *in opinion* opposed to slavery
and to the war, who yet in effect do nothing to put an end
to them; who, esteeming themselves children of Washington
and Franklin, sit down with their hands in their pockets,
and say they know not what to do, and do nothing; who
even postpone the question of freedom to the question of
free-trade, and quietly read the prices-current along with
the latest advices from Mexico. . . . What is the price-
current of an honest man and a patriot today? They
hesitate, and they regret, and sometimes they petition; but
they do nothing in earnest and with effect. They will wait,
well disposed, for others to remedy the evil, that they may
no longer have it to regret. . . .

Oh for a man who is a *man*, and . . . has a bone in his back which you cannot pass your hand through!

I know this well, that if one thousand, if one hundred, if ten men whom I could name, – if ten *honest* men only, – aye, if one HONEST man, in this state of Massachusetts, *ceasing to hold slaves*, were actually to withdraw from this copartnership, and be locked up in the county jail therefor, it would be the abolition of slavery in America. . . .

Under a government which imprisons any unjustly, the true place for a just man is also a prison. The proper place today, the only place which Massachusetts has provided for her freer and less desponding spirits, is in her prisons. . . . It is there that the fugitive slave, and the Mexican prisoner on parole, and the Indian come to plead the wrongs of his race, should find them; on that separate, but more free and honorable ground, where the State places those who are not *with* her but *against* her, – the only house in a slave-state in which a free man can abide with honor. If any think that their influence would be lost there, and their voices no longer afflict the ear of the State . . . they do not know by how much truth is stronger than error, nor how much more eloquently and effectively he can combat injustice who has experienced a little in his own person. . . . But even supposing blood should flow. Is there not a sort of blood shed when the conscience is wounded? Through this wound a man's real manhood and immortality flow out, and he bleeds to an everlasting death. I see this blood flowing now.

Henry Thoreau, 'On the Duty of Civil Disobedience', 1849

❧∘❧

This is my short report from a Moscow nuthouse. On the fifth of August, the Soviet secret security men destroyed anti-war exhibit. Eighty-eight pictures on which I was working for many years were confiscated and probably they will be destroyed. On the 6th of August I was arrested by KGB men who conveyed me to a nuthouse. As I said, I was conveyed to a Moscow nuthouse. They wanted to destroy the idea of peace and disarmament by destroying my ability to paint but the destruction . . . [garbled]. Right now it's hard for me to speak because they are giving me strong drugs. I'm going to fight for peace no matter what. I'm going to do everything I can in order to fight for peace even in these conditions . . . Help me somehow if you can.

Sergei Batovrin, from a cassette tape smuggled out
of a Moscow hospital, August 1982

YOU HAVE BEEN MISLED BY FALSE REPORTS OF WESTERN MASS MEDIA STOP NOT A SINGLE PERSON REPRESENTING PEACE MOVEMENT IN SOVIET UNION IS BEING REPRESSED AND OF COURSE NO ONE OF THEM HAS EVER BEEN ARRESTED. . . . AS FOR TINY GROUP OF ELEVEN PEOPLE PICTURED BY WESTERN PRESS AS INDEPENDENT PEACE MOVEMENT. . . . EYE AM NOT ACQUAINTED WITH ANY OF THEM STOP EYE WAS INFORMED THAT TWO OF THESE PEOPLE . . . HAD BEATEN A WOMAN IN A BUS AND WERE SENTENCED BY DISTRICT PEOPLES COURT TO FIFTEEN DAYS ON CHARGES OF HOOLIGANISM STOP YOU QUALIFY THEIR BEHAVIOUR AS EXAMPLE OF INDEPENDENT STRUGGLE FOR PEACE STOP EYE WOULD CALL IT FLAGRANT BREACH OF PEACE BUT OF COURSE EYE CANNOT INSIST THAT YOUR VIEW OF WHAT IS GOOD AND WHAT IS EVIL COINCIDE WITH MINE STOP.

Cable received from Yuri Zhukov, chairman of the Soviet
Peace Committee, in response to protests from Western
peace groups at the imprisonment of Professor
Medvedkov and Professor Khronopulo, July 1982

Perchance he for whom this bell tolls may be so ill as that he knows not it tolls for him. And perchance I may think myself so much better than I am, as that they who are about me, and see my state, may have called it to toll for me, and I know not that. . . . The bell doth toll for him that thinks it doth. . . . No man is an island, entire of itself; every man is a piece of the continent, a part of the main; if a clod be washed away by the sea, Europe is the less, as well as if a promontory were, as well as if a manor of thy friends or of thine own were; any man's death diminishes me, because I am involved in mankind. And therefore never send to know for whom the bell tolls. It tolls for thee.

John Donne, *Devotions upon Emergent Occasions*, 1624

This life is not a joke
You must take it seriously,
Seriously enough to find yourself
Up against a wall, maybe, with your wrists bound.

Nazim Hikmet, 'Of Life', 1950

'As a woman I have given birth to life; as a teacher, I have nurtured new generations of human beings; as an agriculturalist, I love nature and want to enrich it. . . . Yes, I was amongst the founders of the Peace Association. . . .'
– Reha Isvan, Women's rights campaigner, educationalist and agriculturalist

'Those before you in the dock have served the Turkish state with distinction for a total of 406 years. The prosecutor asks for gaol sentences totalling 500 years. . . . The underlying intention is to deter Turkish intellectuals from espousing the cause of peace and nuclear disarmament. . . .'
– Mahmut Dikerdem, Turkish diplomat, Professor of International Relations

'It is the honour-bound duty of scientists, jurists, or plain citizens to alert public opinion to the dangers of nuclear war. . . . I therefore return the accusations of 'forming an illegal organization' and 'subversion' with my profound regret and revulsion to whence they emanated from. . . .'
– Orhan Apaydin, Member of Turkish Parliament, lawyer, President of the Istanbul Bar Association

Speeches of the leaders of the Turkish Peace Association,
on trial before a Turkish military tribunal, June 1982

❧⊙❧

Hier stehe ich. Ich kann nicht anders. (Here I stand. I can do no other.)

Martin Luther, 1521

❧⊙❧

There is, perhaps, no *woman*, whether she have borne children, or be merely a potential child-bearer, who could look down on a battlefield covered with the slain, but the thought would rise in her, 'So many mothers' sons! So many bodies brought into the world to lie there! So many months of weariness and pain while bones and muscles were shaped within; . . . so many baby mouths drawing life at women's breasts; – all this, that men might lie with glazed eyeballs, and swollen bodies, and fixed, blue, unclosed mouths, and great limbs tossed – this, that an acre of ground might be manured with human flesh!'

140

In a besieged city, it might well happen that men in the streets might seize upon statues and marble carvings from public buildings and galleries and hurl them in to stop the breaches made in their ramparts by the enemy. . . not valuing them more than if they had been paving stones. But one man could not do this – the sculptor! He, who, though there might be no work of his own chisel among them, yet knew what each of these works of art had cost, knew by experience the long years of struggle and study and the infinitude of toil which had gone to the shaping of even one limb, to the carving of even one perfected outline, *he* could never so use them without thought or care. . . . Men's bodies are our women's works of art. Given to us power of control, we will never carelessly throw them in to fill up the gaps in human relationships made by international ambitions and greeds. . . .

War will pass when intellectual culture and activity have made possible to the female an equal share in the governance of modern national life; it will probably not pass away much sooner; its extinction will not be delayed much longer.

It is especially in the domain of war that we, the bearers of men's bodies, who supply its most valuable munition, who, not amid the clamour and ardour of battle, but, singly, and alone, with a three-in-the-morning courage, shed our blood and face death that the battlefield may have its food, a food more precious to us than our heart's blood; it is we especially, who in the domain of war, have our word to say, a word no man can say for us. It is our intention to enter into the domain of war and to labour there till in the course of generations we have extinguished it.

Olive Schreiner, *Woman and Labour*, 1911

Shall there be womanly times, or shall we die?

Ian McEwan, *Or Shall We Die?*, 1983

❧◦❧

Silence, said Nadezhda Mandelstam, is the real crime. In Russian her name *nadezhda* means *hope*. The hope lies in hope. Just as despair can be a self-fulfilling prophecy, so can its opposite. Hope, too, will create its own object – by giving us the strength of mind and voice to tackle our embarassment, our helplessness, our own dark images of death, and come through to a world not merely of our making but of our choosing.

When Lord Mountbatten asks 'Do any of those responsible for this disastrous course pull themselves together and reach for the brakes?' the answer must be 'Watch me!' And the answer 'No' can be reserved for a different question, the question Jacob Bronowski asked at the end of his essay, 'Science and Human Values'. 'Has science fastened on our society a monstrous gift of destruction which we can neither undo nor master, and which like a clockwork automaton is set to break our necks?' No. The bomb is not an uncontrollable automaton, and we are not uncontrolling people.

Our control lies – as it always has done *whenever it's been tried* – in the force of public argument and public anger. It was public opinion in this country which forced the ending of the slave trade – opinion marshalled then as it can be now by pamphlets, speeches and meetings in every village hall. It was fear of the public's outcry which prevented President Nixon from using an atom bomb in Vietnam, and it was the protests of the American people against that cruel and pointless war which eventually secured the American withdrawal. . . .

We forget sometimes our own power. In this country

every penny spent on armaments is money *we* subscribe, every acre of grass behind every barbed-wire fence round every bomber base is an acre of *our* land, and every decision taken by every Minister of State is a decision made on our behalf by a representative elected to *our* service. If those we entrust to manage our affairs adopt strange policies; if they turn out, in office, to be double agents – one hand to pat our babies, the other raised in salute to the Bomb – then we have the right and the duty to dismiss them as unfit.

What happens when an irresistible force meets a *movable* object? Why, it moves.

Nicholas Humphrey, 'Four Minutes to Midnight', 1981

I am a great inventor, did you but know it. . . .
Mine are the battle-ships of righteousness and integrity –
The armor-plates of a quiet conscience and self-respect –
The impregnable conning-tower of divine manhood –
The Long Toms of persuasion –
The machine guns of influence and example –
The dum-dum bullets of pity and remorse –
The impervious cordon of sympathy –
The concentration camps of brotherhood –
The submarine craft of forgiveness –
The Torpedo-boat-destroyer of love –
And behind them all the dynamite of truth!
I do not patent my inventions.
Take them. They are free to all the world.

Ernest H. Crosby, 'War and Hell', 1898

One of the rare glimmers of humanity and reason in the history of Eichmann's patient labors to exterminate the Jews, was the nonviolent resistance offered by the entire nation of Denmark against Nazi power mobilized for genocide.

Denmark was not the only nation that *disagreed* with Hitler on this point. But it was one of the only nations which offered explicit, formal and successful nonviolent resistance to Nazi power. . . . The entire Danish nation simply refused to cooperate with the Nazis, and resisted every move of the Nazis against the Jews with nonviolent resistance of the highest and most effective caliber, yet without any need for organization, training or specialized activism: simply by unanimously and effectively expressing in word and action the force of their deeply held moral convictions. These moral convictions were nothing heroic or sublime. They were merely *ordinary*.

There had of course been subtle and covert refusals on the part of other nations. Italians in particular, while outwardly complying with Hitler's policy, often arranged to help the Jews evade capture or escape from unlocked freight cars. The Danish nation, from the King on down, formally and publicly rejected the policy and opposed it with an open, calm, convinced resistance which shook the morale of the German troops and SS men occupying the country and changed their whole outlook on the Jewish question.

When the Germans first approached the Danes about the segregation of Jews, proposing the introduction of the yellow badge, the government officials replied that the King of Denmark would be the first to wear the badge, and that the introduction of any anti-Jewish measures would lead immediately to their own resignation.

At the same time, the Danes refused to make any distinction between Danish and non-Danish Jews. That is to say, they took the German Jewish refugees under their protection and refused to deport them back to Germany – an act which considerably disrupted the efficiency of Eichmann's organization and delayed anti-Jewish operations until 1943 when Hitler personally ordered that the 'final solution' go into effect without further postponement.

The Danes replied by strikes, by refusals to repair German ships in their shipyards, and by demonstrations of protest. The Germans then imposed martial law. But now it was realized that the German officials in Denmark were changed men. They could 'no longer be trusted'. They refused to cooperate in the liquidation of the Jews, not of course by open protest, but by delays, evasions, covert refusals and the raising of bureaucratic obstacles. . . .

The whole Eichmann story, as told by Hannah Arendt (indeed as told by anybody) acquires a quality of hallucinatory awfulness from the way in which we see how people in many ways exactly like ourselves, claiming as we do to be Christians or at least to live by humanistic standards which approximate, in theory, to the Christian ethic, were able to rationalize a conscious, uninterrupted and complete cooperation in activities which we now see to have been not only criminal but diabolical. Most of the rationalizing probably boiled down to the usual half-truths: 'What can you do? There is no other way out, it is a necessary evil. True, we recognize this kind of action to be in many ways "unpleasant". We hate to take measures like these: but then those at the top know best. It is for the common good . . . and so on.'

Curiously, the Danish exception, while relieving the otherwise unmitigated horror of the story, actually adds to the . . . incredulousness one gets while reading it. After all, the Danes were not even running a special kind of nonviolent movement. They were simply acting according to ordinary beliefs which everybody in Europe theoretically possessed, but which, for some reason, nobody acted on. Quite the contrary! Why did a course of action which worked so simply and so well in Denmark not occur to all the other so-called Christian nations of the West just as simply and just as spontaneously?

Obviously there is no simple answer. It does not even necessarily follow that the Danes are men of greater faith or deeper piety than other western Europeans. But perhaps it is true that these people had been less perverted and secularized by the emptiness and cynicism, the thought-lessness, the crude egoism and the rank amorality which have become characteristic of our world, even where we still see an apparent surface of Christianity. It is not so much that the Danes were Christians, as that they were *human*.

Thomas Merton, 'Danish Nonviolent
Resistance to Hitler', 1971

⬥∘⬥

Who are you?
Well, I'm everybody who's nobody.
I'm the nobody who's everybody.
What's your racket?
What do you do for a living?
Well, I'm an engineer, musician,
Streetcleaner, carpenter, teacher,
How about a farmer?
  Also!
Office clerk?
  Yes ma'am!
Mechanic?
  That's right.
Housewife?

Certainly.
Factory worker?
  You said it.
Stenographer?
  H'um-h'um!
Union specialist?
  Positively!
Truck driver?
  Definitely.
Writer, teacher, preacher?
  All of them.
  I am the etcetera.
Are you an American?
I'm just an Irish, Negro, Jewish,
Italian, French, and English,
Spanish, Russian, Chinese,
Polish, Scotch, Hungarian,
Litvak, Swedish, Finnish,
Canadian, Greek and Turk,
And Czech and double-check American:

Out of the cheating, out of the shooting,
Out of the murders and lynching,
Out of the windbags, the patriotic spouting,
Out of uncertainty and doubting and
Out of the carpet-bag and the brass spittoon,
It will come again – our marching song will come again,
Simple as a hit tune, deep as our valleys,
High as our mountains, strong as the people who made it.

                    Paul Robeson and Earl Robinson,
                    'Ballad for Americans', 1939

They cut me down, and I leapt up high;
For I am the life that'll never die;
I'll live in you if you'll live in me;
For I am the Lord of the Dance, said he.

Anon

❖⊃∘⊂❖

MY DEAR FELLOW CLERGYMEN: While confined here in the Birmingham city jail, I came across your recent statement calling my present activities 'unwise and untimely'. . . . I had hoped that the white moderate would reject the myth concerning time in relation to the struggle for freedom. I have just received a letter from a white brother in Texas. He writes: 'All Christians know that the colored people will receive equal rights eventually, but it is possible that you are in too great a religious hurry. It has taken Christianity almost two thousand years to accomplish what it has. The teachings of Christ take time to come to earth.' Such an attitude stems from a tragic misconception of time, from the strangely irrational notion that there is something in the very flow of time that will eventually cure all ills. Actually, time itself is neutral; it can be used either destructively or constructively. More and more I feel that the people of ill will have used time much more effectively than have the people of good will. We will have to repent in this generation not merely for the hateful words and actions of the bad people, but for the appalling silence of the good people. Human progress never rolls in on wheels of inevitability; it comes through the tireless efforts of men willing to be co-workers with God, and without this hard work, time itself becomes an ally of the forces of social stagnation. We must use time creatively, in the knowledge that the time is always ripe to do right.

Martin Luther King Jr, 'Letter from Birmingham Jail' 1965

❖⊃∘⊂❖

9

In a Dark Time

In the beginning God created the heaven and the earth. And the earth was without form and void; and darkness was upon the face of the deep. And the Spirit of God moved upon the face of the waters. And God said, Let there be light: and there was light.

Genesis 1:1–3

We did not choose to live in this time. But there is no way of getting out of it. And it has given to us as significant a cause as has ever been known, a moment of opportunity which might never be renewed. . . . The opportunity is *now*, when there is already an enhanced consciousness of danger informing millions. We can match this crisis only by a summoning of resources to a height like that of the greatest religious or political movements of Europe's past. I think, once again, of 1944 and of the crest of the Resistance. There must be that kind of spirit abroad in Europe once more. But this time it must arise, not in the wake of war and repression, but before these take place. Five minutes afterwards and it will be too late.

Humankind must at last grow up. We must recognize that the Other is ourselves.

Edward Thompson, *Beyond the Cold War*, 1982

It is not love to my neighbour – whom I often do not know at all – which induces me to seize a pail of water and rush towards his house when I see it on fire; it is a far wider, even though more vague feeling or instinct of human solidarity and sociability which moves me. . . . It is not love, and not even sympathy which induces a herd of ruminants or of horses to form a ring in order to resist an attack of wolves; not love which induces wolves to form a pack for hunting; not love which induces kittens or lambs to play, or a dozen of species of young birds to spend their days together in autumn. It is a feeling infinitely wider than love or personal sympathy – an instinct that has been slowly developed among animals and men in the course of an extremely long evolution, and which has taught animals and men alike the force they can borrow from the practice of mutual aid and support, and the joys they can find in social life. . . .

Love, sympathy and self-sacrifice certainly play an immense part in the progressive development of our moral feelings. But it is not love and not even sympathy upon which Society is based in mankind. It is the conscience – be it only at the stage of an instinct – of human solidarity. It is the unconscious recognition of . . . the close dependency of every one's happiness upon the happiness of all; and of the sense of justice, or equity, which brings the individual to consider the rights of every other individual as equal to his own.

Petr Kropotkin, Mutual Aid, 1902

✑◦⇐

We cannot continue in this paralysing mistrust. If we want to work our way out of the desperate situation in which we find ourselves another spirit must enter into the people. It can only come if the awareness of its necessity suffices to give us strength to believe in its coming. We must presuppose the awareness of this need in all the peoples who have suffered along with us. We must approach them in the spirit that we are human beings, all of us, and that we feel ourselves fitted to feel with each other; to think and to will together in the same way. . . .

The awareness that we are all human beings together has become lost in war and through politics. We have reached the point of regarding each other only as members of a people either allied with us or against us. . . . Now we must rediscover the fact that we – all together – are human beings, and we must strive to concede to each other what moral capacity we have. Only in this way can we begin to believe that in other peoples as well as in ourselves there will arise the need for a new spirit. . . .

At this stage we have the choice of two risks: the one lies in continuing the mad atomic arms race; . . . the other in the renunciation of nuclear weapons, and in the hope that America and the Soviet Union, and the peoples associated with them, will manage to live in peace. The first holds no hope of a prosperous future; the second does. We must risk the second.

Albert Schweitzer, *Peace or Atomic War?*, 1958

❧◦☙

We face a new dimension of destruction – not a matter of disaster or even of a war – but rather of an end.

We reject that nuclear end. We believe in – commit ourselves to – the flow and continuity of human life, and to the products of human imagination.

We believe in the possibility of collective human power on behalf of change, awareness, and ultimately on behalf of human survival.

We believe in the possibility of a non-nuclear world – a world that reasserts the great chain of being and directs its energies toward humane goals.

We recognize that our own lives must be inevitably and profoundly bound up with this struggle.

In confronting the threat rather than numbing ourselves to it, we experience greater vitality. We feel stronger human ties. We turn to beauty, love, spirituality, and sensuality. We touch the earth and we touch each other.

153

In struggling to preserve humankind we experience a renewed sense of human possibility in general. We feel part of prospective historical and evolutionary achievements. We feel not only ourselves but our species, and relationship to the species, to be newly alive.

Robert Jay Lifton, 'A Nuclear Age Ethos', 1983

❧⊙❧

The fateful question for the human species [is] whether and to what extent their cultural development will succeed in mastering the disturbance of their communal life by the human instinct of aggression and self-destruction. It may be that in this respect precisely the present time deserves a special interest. Men have gained control over the forces of nature to such an extent that with their help they would have no difficulty in exterminating one another to the last man. They know this, and hence comes a large part of their current unrest, their unhappiness and their mood of anxiety. And now it is to be expected that the other of the two 'Heavenly Powers', eternal Eros, will make an effort to assert himself in the struggle with his equally immortal adversary [Thanatos].

Sigmund Freud, 'Civilization and its Discontents', 1931

❧⊙❧

I have set before you life and death, blessing and cursing; therefore choose life, that both thou and thy seed may live.

Deuteronomy 30:19

❧⊙❧

Some say a cavalry corps,
some infantry, some, again,
will maintain that the swift oars

of our fleet are the finest
sight on dark earth; but I say
that whatever one loves, is.

Sappho, 'To an Army Wife in Sardis', 7th century BC

We are now speeding inexorably towards a day when even the ingenuity of our scientists may be unable to save us from the consequences of a single rash act or a lone reckless hand upon the switch of an uninterceptible missile. For twelve years now we've sought to stave off this ultimate threat of disaster by devising arms which would be both ultimate and disastrous.

This irony can probably be compounded a few more years, or perhaps even a few decades. Missiles will bring anti-missiles, and anti-missiles will bring anti-anti-missiles. But inevitably, this whole electronic house of cards will reach a point where it can be constructed no higher.

At that point we shall have come to the peak of this whole incredible dilemma into which the world is shoving itself. And when that time comes there will be little we can do other than to settle down uneasily, smother our fears, and attempt to live in a thickening shadow of death. . . .

Have we already gone too far in this search for peace through the accumulation of peril? Is there any way to halt this trend – or must we push on with new devices until we inevitably come to judgment before the atom? I believe there is a way out . . . [But] until we get started, we shall never know what can be done.

Omar N. Bradley, General of the Army,
speech in Washington, 1957

As a military man who has given half a century of active service I say in all sincerity that the nuclear arms race has no military purpose. Wars cannot be fought with nuclear weapons. Their existence only adds to our perils because of the illusions they have generated.

There are powerful voices around the world who still give credence to the old Roman precept – if you desire peace, prepare for war. This is absolute nuclear nonsense and I repeat – it is a disastrous misconception to believe that by increasing the total uncertainty one increases one's own certainty. . . .

Science offers us almost unlimited opportunities, but it is up to us, the people, to make the moral and philosophical choices. And since the threat to humanity is the work of human beings, it is up to man to save himself from himself.

The world now stands on the brink of the final Abyss. Let us all resolve to take all possible practical steps to ensure that we do not, through our own folly, go over the edge.

> Earl Mountbatten, Admiral of the Fleet, speech at
> Strasbourg, May 1979

It's not all that complicated. The United States has been leading the arms race by three to five years since we developed the atomic bomb, the hydrogen bomb, right up through today's Cruise missiles and the Pershing. We've been leading that arms race. If the United States and the people of the United States are serious about reducing the threat of nuclear war and slowing, reversing, and stopping the arms race, they simply have to take action here in the United States with our own Congress, with our own elected officials throughout our government. We don't have to think that somebody else is going to solve this problem. I think it's a kind of cop-out to suggest that the solution lies in some big world organization. The solution lies here in the hearts and minds and actions of the American public. We can slow, stop, and reverse that arms race when we make up our minds to do it.

Admiral Gene LaRocque, interview, 1982

❧❀❧

Why do we address these matters fraught with such complexity, controversy and passion? We speak as pastors, not politicians. We are teachers, not technicians. We cannot avoid our responsibility to lift up the moral dimensions of the choices before our world and nation. The nuclear age is an era of moral as well as physical danger. We are the first generation since Genesis with the power to threaten the created order. We cannot remain silent in the face of such danger. Why do we address these issues? We are simply trying to live up to the call of Jesus to be peacemakers in our own time and situation.

What are we saying? Fundamentally, we are saying that the decisions about nuclear weapons are among the most pressing moral questions of our age. While these decisions have obvious military and political aspects, they involve fundamental moral choices. In simple terms, we are saying that good ends (defending one's country, protecting freedom, etc.) cannot justify immoral means (the use of weapons which kill indiscriminately and threaten whole societies). We fear that our world and nation are headed in the wrong direction. More weapons with greater destructive potential are produced every day. More and more nations are seeking to become nuclear powers. In our quest for more and more security we are actually becoming less and less secure.

157

In the words of our Holy Father, we need a 'moral about-face'. The whole world must summon the moral courage and technical means to say no to nuclear conflict; no to weapons of mass destruction; no to an arms race which robs the poor and the vulnerable; and no to the moral danger of a nuclear age which places before human-kind indefensible choices of constant terror or surrender. Peacemaking is not an optional commitment. It is a requirement of our faith.

US Catholic Bishops' letter, 'The Challenge of Peace', 1983

Seek not death in the error of your life; and pull not upon yourselves destruction with the works of your hands. For God made not death: neither hath he pleasure in the destruction of the living. For he created all things, that they might have their being; and the generations of the world were healthful; and there is no poison of destruction in them, nor the kingdom of death upon the earth.

The Wisdom of Solomon 1:12–14

The sap is mounting back from that unseenness
darkly renewing in the common deep,
back to the light, and feeding the pure greenness
hiding in rinds round which the winds still weep.

Rainer Maria Rilke, 'The Sap is Mounting Back', 1924

I look into the air and find the spaces where our children's children might be; among the rain and the sun and the leaves those bodies are realizable; and I feel with a terrible hope how lovely life is – and how unbearable is the thought that by our own blindness, by our lack of memory and courage, by our slackness we could end it.

Susannah York, speech in Trafalgar Square, October 1980

In a dark time, the eye begins to see.

Theodore Roethke, 'In a Dark Time', 1966

Index of Contributors

Index of Contributors

Sources and Acknowledgements

For permission to reprint copyright material the editors and publishers gratefully acknowledge the owners of copyright in the works and extracts included in this anthology.

Dannie Abse. Poem adapted from the Hebrew of Amir Gilboa, *Way Out in the Center*. London: Hutchinson Publishing Group Ltd, 1982.
American Infantryman, *see* Lifton, *Home from the War*.
Jean Anouilh. *Antigone*, trans. Lewis Galantière. New York: Random House, Inc.; London: Methuen and Co. Ltd, 1960, pp. 34–5. Reprinted by permission.
Orhan Apaydin, *see* Furtado, *Turkey*.
Louis Aragon. Dada Manifesto. In Maurice Nadeau, *The History of Surrealism*, trans. Richard Howard, Paris: Editions du Seuil; London: Jonathan Cape Ltd, 1968, p. 62. Reprinted by permission of the publishers.
Antonin Artaud. 'On Suicide', *Artaud Anthology*, ed. Jack Hirschman. San Francisco: City Lights Books, 1965. Copyright © 1965 by City Lights Books. Reprinted by permission.
Atom test observer, *see* Scheer, *With Enough Shovels*.
W. H. Auden. *For the Time Being: A Christmas Oratorio*. New York: Random House, Inc.; London: Faber & Faber Ltd, 1944. Copyright 1944 and renewed © 1972 by W. H. Auden. Reprinted from *W. H. Auden: Collected Poems*, ed. Edward Mendelson, by permission of the publishers.
Sergei Batovrin. Cassette tape, made by Natasha Batovrin on 13 August 1982 in Moscow Psychoneurological Hospital No. 14, and smuggled out of Soviet Union. By permission of Sergei Batovrin.
Ernest Becker. *Escape from Evil*. New York: The Free Press, 1975, pp. 110–11. Copyright © 1975 by Marie Becker. Extracts reprinted with permission of The Free Press, a division of Macmillan, Inc.
Patrick Blackett. Quoted by Horst-Eberhard Richter, 'Living under the Threat of Nuclear War', *The Human Cost of Nuclear*

War, ed. Stephen Farrow and Alex Chown. Cardiff: Medical Campaign against Nuclear Weapons, 1983, p. 99.

William Blake. 'The Divine Image', 'The Little Boy Lost', 'Introduction: Songs of Innocence', *William Blake: Poems and Prophecies*, ed. Max Plowman. London: J. M. Dent & Sons Ltd., 1975.

Alexander Blok. 'The Kite', *Poems from the Russian*, trans. Frances Cornford and Esther Polianowsky Salaman. London: Faber & Faber Ltd, 1943, p. 58. Reprinted by permission of the publisher.

Tadeusz Borowski. 'The Death of Schillinger', *This Way to the Gas, Ladies and Gentlemen*, trans. Barbara Vedder. New York: Viking Penguin Inc.; Harmondsworth: Penguin Books Ltd, 1967, pp. 145–6. Copyright © 1959 by Maria Borowski. This translation copyright © 1967 by Penguin Books Ltd. Reprinted by permission of the publishers.

Peter G. Bourne. 'From Boot Camp to My Lai', *Crimes of War*, ed. Richard Falk, Gabriel Kolko and Robert Jay Lifton. New York: Random House, Inc., 1971, p. .463. Reprinted by permission.

Omar Bradley, General of the Army, Speech quoted in Gwyn Prins, ed., *Defended to Death*. Harmondsworth: Penguin Books, 1983, pp. 294–5. Reprinted by permission of Penguin Books Ltd.

Bertolt Brecht. From *Mother Courage*, trans. by Eric Bentley. London: Methuen and Co. Ltd, 1962, Random House Original Work © 1949 by Suhrkamp Verlag, Frankfurt-am-Main. Translation © 1955, 1959, 1961, 1962 by Eric Bentley. Reprinted by permission of Suhrkamp and Methuen.

John Buchan. *Francis and Riversdale Grenfell*. London: Nelson, 1920, p. 189. Reprinted by permission of the Rt. Hon. Lord Tweedsmuir, CBE.

Samuel Butler. *Notebooks*, ed. Geoffrey Keynes and Brian Hill. London: Jonathan Cape Ltd, 1951, p. 193.

Albert Camus. 'Combat', *Actuelles: Ecrits politiques*. Paris: © Editions Gallimard, 1977, pp. 67–8. (Translation by Nicholas Humphrey.) Reprinted by permission of the publisher.

Walter Cannon. 'Voodoo Death', *American Anthropologist*, 44 (1942), 169–81. Reprinted by permission of the American Anthropological Association.

Hadley Cantril. *The Invasion from Mars: A Study in the Psychology of Panic*. Princeton, NJ: Princeton University Press, 1940, pp. 47, 96–7. Copyright 1940, copyright © renewed by Princeton University Press. Reprinted by permission.

T. Carmi. 'Author's Apology', *Anatomy of a War*, 1977. © by T. Carmi. All rights reserved. Reprinted by permission of the author and ACUM Ltd.

Angela Carter. 'Angler in a Black Landscape', *Over Our Dead Bodies*, ed. Dorothy Thompson. London: Virago Press, 1983, pp. 154–5. Reprinted by permission.

Catholic Bishops. *The Challenge of Peace: God's Promise and Our Response*, §331, §332, §333. Copyright © 1983 by the United States Catholic Conference, Washington, DC. All rights reserved. Used by permission.

C. P. Cavafy. 'Waiting for the Barbarians', *C. P. Cavafy: Collected Poems*, ed. George Savidis, trans. Edmund Keeley and Philip Sherrard. Princeton, NJ: Princeton University Press; London, Chatto & Windus Ltd, 1975. Reprinted by permission of the publishers.

Paul Celan. 'Speak, You Also', *Paul Celan: Poems*, trans. Michael Hamburger. New York: Persea Books, 1980, p. 85. Copyright © 1980 by Michael Hamburger. Reprinted by permission of the publisher and the translator.

Paul Chilton. 'Nukespeak', *Undercurrents*, 48 (1982), 12. Reprinted by permission of Paul Chilton.

Eric Chivian, MD, and Roberta Snow. 'There's a Nuclear War Going On Inside Me' (videotape of interviews with children in Massachusetts schools). Copyright © 1983 by International Physicians for the Prevention of Nuclear War, Boston, Mass. Used by permission of Eric Chivian, MD. Reprinted in *The Human Cost of Nuclear War*, ed. Stephen Farrow and Alex Crown, 1983, pp. 109, 112–13. Reprinted by permission of Eric Chivan, MD, and Stephen Farrow.

Eric Chivian, MD, John E. Mack, MD, and Jeremy Waletzky, MD. 'What Soviet Children are Saying about Nuclear Weapons' (videotape of interview with Soviet children). Copyright © 1983 by International Physicians for the Prevention of Nuclear War, Boston, Mass. Used by permission of John E. Mack, MD, and Eric Chivian, MD.

Winston Churchill. Recently declassified memorandum. Quoted by Kovel, *Against the State of Nuclear Terror*.

A. Clutton-Brock. 'Christmas 1914', from 'More Thoughts on the War', quoted in Arthur Stanley, ed., *The Seven Stars of Peace*. London: J. M. Dent & Sons Ltd, 1940, p. 81.

Ernest Crosby. 'War and Hell', *Swords and Plowshares*. New York: Funk & Wagnalls, 1902; London: Grant Richards, 1903.

Daily Express, August 1981 quotation. Reprinted by permission of the publisher.

Daily Worker, August 1945 quotations. Reprinted by permission of *Morning Star*.

Robert James Dalby. *Tight Corners*. London: George Allen & Unwin Ltd, 1940. Reprinted by permission of the publishers.

Mahmut Dikerdem, *see* Furtado, *Turkey*.

John Donne. *Devotions upon Emergent Occasions*.

John Dos Passos. 'The Body of an American', 'The Big Money', *USA Nineteen Nineteen*. Boston: Houghton Mifflin; Harmondsworth: Penguin Books Ltd., 1966, pp. 722–3, 1080. Reprinted by permission of Elizabeth H. Dos Passos.

Bob Dylan. 'Talkin' World War III Blues'. Quoted in *Bob Dylan: Writings and Drawings*. © 1963 Warner Bros. Inc. All rights reserved. Used by permission of Warner Bros. Music.

Eleven-year-old girl, *see* Chivian and Snow, 'There's a Nuclear War Going On Inside Me'.

Thomas Farrell. Quoted in Leslie R. Groves, *Now It Can Be Told: The Story of the Manhattan Project*. New York: Harper & Row, Inc., 1962, pp. 437–8.

Jerome D. Frank. 'Prenuclear-Age Leaders and the Nuclear Arms Race', *American Journal of Orthopsychiatry*, 52 (1982), 633. Copyright 1982 by the American Orthopsychiatric Association, Inc. Reprinted by permission of the author and publisher.

James L. Franklin. 'The Religious Right and the New Apocalypse', *Boston Globe*, 2 May 1982. Reprinted courtesy of the *Boston Globe*.

Sigmund Freud. 'Thoughts for the Times on War and Death', *The Standard Edition of the Complete Psychological Works of Sigmund Freud*, vol. 14, trans. James Strachey. London: The Hogarth Press Ltd, 1915. *The Collected Papers of Sigmund Freud*, vol. IV. New York: Basic Books, Inc., 1959. Reprinted by permission of Sigmund Freud Copyrights Ltd, the Institute of Psycho-Analysis and the publishers.

Sigmund Freud. 'Civilization and its Discontents', *The Standard*

Edition of the Complete Psychological Works of Sigmund Freud, vol. 21, trans. James Strachey. New York: W. W. Norton & Company, Inc.; London: The Hogarth Press Ltd, 1930. Reprinted by permission of Sigmund Freud Copyrights Ltd, the Institute of Psycho-Analysis and the publishers.

Erich Fromm. *The Anatomy of Human Destructiveness*. New York: Holt, Rinehart & Winston, Inc.; London: Jonathan Cape Ltd, 1974, pp. 350–1. Reprinted by permission of Erich Fromm Estate and the publishers.

Jean Furtado, ed. *Turkey: Peace on Trial*. London: Merlin Press Ltd, 1983. Reprinted by permission.

Francis Gasquet. *The Great Pestilence*, 1893.

German Eyewitness, *see* Hilberg, *The Destruction of the European Jews*.

German Press, *see* Hilberg, *The Destruction of the European Jews*.

Edward Glover. *War, Sadism and Pacifism*. London: George Allen & Unwin Ltd, 1946, p. 274. Reprinted by permission.

Günter Grass. *The Tin Drum*, trans. Ralph Manheim. New York: Alfred A. Knopf; London: Martin Secker & Warburg Ltd, 1965, pp. 110, 114. Reprinted by permission of the publishers.

Colin Gray. Quoted by the *Washington Post*, 16 April, 1982.

Riversdale Grenfell, *see* Buchan, *Francis and Riversdale Grenfell*.

M. Hachiya. *Hiroshima Diary*, trans. and ed. Warner Wells. Chapel Hill: University of North Carolina Press, 1955, p. 70. Reprinted by permission.

Bill Haley, *see* Dickie Thompson.

Thomas Hardy. 'The Man He Killed'.

Joseph Heller. *Catch 22*. New York: Simon & Schuster Inc.; London: Jonathan Cape Ltd, 1961, pp. 446–7, 450. Copyright © 1955, 1961, by Joseph Heller. Reprinted by permission of the author and publishers.

Herodotus. *Herodotus: A New and Literal Translation*, trans. by Henry Cary. London: George Bell, 1879.

Nazim Hikmet. 'Of Life', *see* Furtado, *Turkey*.

Raul Hilberg. *The Destruction of the European Jews*. London: W. H. Allen & Co. Ltd, 1961, pp. 669, 655, 656. Reprinted by permission.

A. V. Hill. 'The Red Army', *The Ethical Dilemma of Science*, New York: Rockefeller University Press, 1960, pp. 285–7. Reprinted by permission.

Hiroshima grocer, *see* Lifton, *Death in Life*.
Hiroshima history professor, *see* Lifton, *Death in Life*.
Hoover Commission. Quoted in Kovel, *Against the State of Nuclear Terror*.
Nicholas Humphrey. 'Four Minutes to Midnight', An Immodest Proposal', *Consciousness Regained*. Oxford: Oxford University Press, 1983. Reprinted by permission.
Aldous Huxley. Unpublished speech delivered at the Albert Hall, 1936. Reprinted by permission of Mrs Laura Huxley and Chatto & Windus Ltd.
David Ignatow. 'A Meditation on Violence', 'Soldier', *Rescue the Dead*. Middletown. Conn.: Wesleyan University Press, 1968. Reprinted by permission.
Eugene Ionesco. 'Journal', *Encounter* (May 1966).
Reha Isvan, *see* Furtado, *Turkey*.
Franz Jägerstätter. From Gordon Zahn, *In Solitary Witness*. New York: Holt, Rinehart & Winston, Inc., 1964. Reprinted by permission of Gordon Zahn.
Alia Johnson. 'Why We Should Drop the Bombs', *Evolutionary Blues*, 1, 1981.
C. G. Jung. From 'Wotan' and 'Epilogue to Essays on Contemporary Events', in *Collected Works*, 10: *Civilization in Transition*, trans. R. F. C. Hull. London: Routledge & Kegan Paul Ltd, 1964. Reprinted by permission.
Ernst Jünger. *Diary*. 1918.
Martin Luther King. 'Letter from Birmingham Jail', *Why We Can't Wait*. London: Harper & Row Ltd, 1965; reprinted by permission of Harper & Row Ltd.
Joel Kovel. *Against the State of Nuclear Terror*. London: Pan Books, 1983. Reprinted by permission.
Petr Kropotkin. *Mutual Aid: A Factor of Evolution*. Boston, Mass.: Porter Sargent Publishers, Inc., 1902.
Lao-tzu. From the Chinese of Lao-tzu (*Tao Tê Ching XXX*), trans. Ernest Crosby. *See* Crosby, *Swords and Plowshares*, p. 10.
Admiral Gene LaRocque. Interview by Stephen Most, in *First Biennial Conference on the Fate of the Earth*. San Francisco: Earth Island Institute, 1982, pp. 427–8. Reprinted Stephen Most, ed., *The Broken Circle*. Used by permission.
Edmund Leach. *Custom, Law and Terrorist Violence*. Edinburgh: Edinburgh University Press. 1977, p. 35. Reprinted by permission.

Edward Lear. *The Complete Nonsense of Edward Lear*, ed. Holbrook Jackson. London: Faber & Faber Ltd, 1947, p. 10.

Tom Lehrer. 'We Will All Go Together When We Go', © 1958 Tom Lehrer, 'So Long, Mom', © 1965 Tom Lehrer, *Too Many Songs by Tom Lehrer with Not Enough Pictures by Ronald Searle*. New York: Pantheon Books; London: Methuen & Co. Ltd, 1981. Used by permission.

Robert Jay Lifton. *Boundaries*. New York: Random House, Inc., 1970, pp. 26–7. Used by permission.

Robert Jay Lifton. *Home from the War*. New York: Simon & Schuster, Inc., 1973; London: Wildwood House, 1974, p. 252. Reissued New York: Basic Books, 1985. Reprinted by permission of Deborah Rogers Ltd, International Creative Management, and Basic Books, Inc.

Robert Jay Lifton. *Death in Life*. New York: Basic Books, 1968, pp. 27, 29. Reissued New York: Basic Books, 1982. © 1967 by Robert Jay Lifton. Reprinted by permission.

Robert Jay Lifton. 'A Nuclear-Age Ethos'. Unpublished.

Robert Jay Lifton. Testimony to Select Committee of the United States House of Representatives, 1983.

Robert Jay Lifton and Kai Erikson. 'Nuclear War's Effect on the Mind.' *New York Times*, 15 March 1982.

Robert Jay Lifton and Richard Falk. *Indefensible Weapons*. New York: Basic Books, 1982, pp. 10–11, 106–7. Reprinted by permission.

Stanley Loomis. *Paris in the Terror: June 1793–July 1794*. London: Jonathan Cape Ltd., 1965, pp. 73, 82. By permission of Stanley P. Loomis Estate.

Robert Lowell. From A. Alvarez, 'A Talk with Robert Lowell', *Encounter*, February 1965, pp. 39–46. Reprinted by permission of *Encounter* and A. Alvarez.

Robert Lowell. 'Fall 1961', *For the Union Dead*. New York: Farrar, Straus & Giroux, Inc.; London: Faber & Faber Ltd, 1964. Copyright © 1962, 1964 by Robert Lowell. Reprinted by permission of the publishers.

Mary McCarthy. *Vietnam*. New York: Harcourt, Brace & World, Inc., 1967.

Ian McEwan. *Or Shall We Die?* London: Jonathan Cape Ltd, 1983, p. 31. Copyright © 1983 by Ian McEwan. From the oratorio by Michael Berkeley and Ian McEwan. Used by permission.

Senator Brien M. McMahon. Speech before the United States Senate. Quoted in Marc Ian Barasch, *The Little Black Book of Atomic War*. New York: Dell Publishing Co., Inc. 1983, p. 45.

John E. Mack. Testimony to Select Committee of the United States House of Representatives, 1983.

Nadezhda Mandelstam. *Hope against Hope,* trans. Max Hayward. New York: Atheneum Publishers, Inc., 1970; London: William Collins Sons & Co. Ltd, 1971, pp. 41–3. © 1970 by Atheneum Publishers. Reprinted by permission of the publishers.

Mao Tse-Tung. Talk with Anna Louise Strong, August 1960.

F. T. Marinetti. Lines from the 'Manifesto of Futurism', *Marinetti: Selected Writings*, ed. R. W. Flint, trans. R. W. Flint and Arthur Coppotelli. New York: Farrar, Straus & Giroux, Inc., 1972. Copyright © 1971, 1972 by Farrar, Straus & Giroux, Inc. Reprinted by permission of the publisher.

Vladimir Mayakovsky. 'I', *Mayakovsky and His Poetry*, trans. George Reavey. Bombay: Current Book House, 1955.

Herman Melville. *Moby Dick*. Harmondsworth: Penguin Books Ltd, 1972, p. 283.

Thomas Merton. 'Danish Nonviolent Resistance to Hitler', *The Nonviolent Alternative*. New York: Farrar, Straus & Giroux, Inc., 1971, pp. 165–7. (Originally published as *Thomas Merton on Peace*.) Copyright © 1971, 1980 by the Trustees of the Merton Legacy Trust. Reprinted by permission of the publishers and the Merton Legacy Trust.

Edna St Vincent Millay, 'Conscientious Objector', *Collected Poems*. New York: Harper & Row, Inc. Copyright 1934, 1962 by Edna St Vincent Millay and Norma Millay Ellis. Reprinted by permission.

John Milton. *Paradise Lost*, Book IX, lines 129–30, 136–9.

Minucius Felix. 'Octavius', quoted by Norman Cohn, *Europe's Inner Demons*. London: Sussex University Press, 1975, p. 1.

Michel de Montaigne. *Essays*, trans. J. M. Cohen. Harmondsworth: Penguin Books Ltd, 1958, p. 326. Copyright © J. M. Cohen, 1958. Reprinted by permission of the publisher.

Earl Mountbatten, Admiral of the Fleet. Speech at Strasbourg, May 1979.

News (Portsmouth), June 1983. Reprinted by permission of the editor.

New York Times, 25 November 1969, 15 March 1982, 23 August

1982. © 1969, 1982 by the New York Times Company. Reprinted by permission.

George Orwell. *Homage to Catalonia*, in *The Collected Essays, Journalism and Letters of George Orwell*, IV, 254, New York: Harcourt Brace Jovanovich, Inc.; London: Martin Secker & Warburg Ltd, 1968. Copyright © 1968 by Sonia Brownell Orwell. Reprinted by permission of the Estate of the late Sonia Brownell Orwell and the publishers.

George Orwell. 'Politics and the English Language', *Shooting an Elephant and Other Essays*. New York: Harcourt Brace Jovanovich, Inc., 1946. Copyright 1946 by Sonia Brownell Orwell; renewed 1974 by Sonia Orwell. Reprinted by permission of the Estate of the late Sonia Brownell Orwell, Martin Secker & Warburg Ltd, and Harcourt Brace Jovanovich, Inc.

Philip Payne, Letter to *The Times*, 22 May 1981. Reprinted by permission of Philip Payne.

Plague survivor, *see* Gasquet, *The Great Pestilence*.

Ronald Reagan, *see* Franklin, 'The Religious Right'.

Henry Reed, 'Naming of Parts', *A Map of Verona*. London: Jonathan Cape Ltd. 1946. Reprinted by permission.

Rainer Maria Rilke. 'The Sap Is Mounting Back from that Unseenness', lines 1–4, *Selected Works*, vol. II, trans. J. B. Leishman. London: The Hogarth Press, 1964, p. 83. Reprinted by permission of St John's College, Oxford, and the publisher.

Paul Robeson and Earl Robinson. 'Ballad for Americans', from Marie Seton, *Paul Robeson*. London: Dobson Books, Ltd, 1958, pp. 129–30. Reprinted by permission of the publisher and Clarke Conway-Gordon.

Rock Music Source Book, ed. Bob Macken, Peter Fornatale, and Bill Ayres. New York: Doubleday & Co., Inc., 1980.

Theodore Roethke. 'In a Dark Time', *The Collected Poems of Theodore Roethke*. New York: Doubleday & Co., Inc.; London: Faber & Faber Ltd, 1966, p. 239. Copyright 1960 by Beatrice Roethke as Administratrix of the Estate of Theodore Roethke. Reprinted by permission.

Bertrand Russell. *Autobiography of Bertrand Russell,* vol. II. London: George Allen & Unwin Ltd, 1968. Reprinted by permission.

Thomas Sackville. 'The Shield of War', lines 1–18.

Sappho. 'To an Army Wife in Sardis', *Sappho: A New Trans-*

171

lation, trans. Mary Barnard. Berkeley & Los Angeles: University of California Press, 1958. Reprinted by permission.

Jean-Paul Sartre. *Existentialism and Humanism*. trans. Philip Mairet. London: Methuen & Co. Ltd, 1960, pp. 29–30. Reprinted by permission of Methuen & Co. Ltd and Philosophical Library, Inc.

George Schaller. *Serengeti: A Kingdom of Predators*. New York: Alfred A. Knopf; London: William Collins Sons & Co. Ltd, 1973, p. 109. Reprinted by permission of the publishers.

Robert Scheer. *With Enough Shovels: Reagan, Bush and Nuclear War*. New York: Random House, Inc., 1982; London: Martin Secker & Warburg Ltd, 1983, pp. 16–17, 31. Reprinted by permission of the publishers.

Arthur Schopenhauer. 'On Suicide', *The Essential Schopenhauer*. London: George Allen & Unwin Ltd, 1962, p. 101. Reprinted by permission.

Olive Schreiner. *Women and Labour*. London: Virago Press Ltd, pp. 170, 173–4, 178. Reprinted by permission of the publisher.

Albert Schweitzer. *Peace or Atomic War?* London: A. & C. Black Ltd, 1958, pp. 26–7. Reprinted by permission of Monsieur Gustav Woytt.

Martin E. P. Seligman. *Helplessness*. San Francisco: W. H. Freeman and Company, 1975, pp. 166–8. Copyright © 1975. Reprinted by permission of the publisher.

Seneca. *Letters*, XCV. In Arthur Stanley, ed., *The Seven Stars of Peace*. London: J. N. Dent & Sons Ltd, 1940, p. 15.

William Shakespeare. *Macbeth*, IV, iii, 164.

Rose Shapiro. 'Terrorism', *Time Out*, 6 February 1981. Reprinted by permission of Time Out Limited.

Soldiers killed in two world wars. Figures from Gwyn Prins, ed., *Defended to Death*. Harmondsworth: Penguin Books Ltd, 1982, p. 50; and Francis A. Beer, *Peace Against War*. San Francisco: W. H. Freeman and Company, 1981, pp. 37–8.

Albert Speer. *Inside the Third Reich: Memoirs of Albert Speer*, trans. R. and C. Winston. London: George Weidenfeld & Nicolson Ltd, 1970. Reprinted by permission.

John Steinbeck. *Once There Was a War*. New York: Viking Penguin Inc., 1958; London: William Heinemann Ltd, 1959, pp. ix, xx. Copyright © 1943, 1958 by John Steinbeck. Copyright renewed © 1971 by Elaine Steinbeck, John Steinbeck IV, and Thom Steinbeck. Reprinted by permission of the publishers and McIntosh and Otis, Inc.

Sun(London), 4 May 1982. Reprinted by permission.

Heinrich Suso. Quoted in Norman Cohn, *The Pursuit of the Millennium*. London: Paladin, 1970, p. 127.

Dylan Thomas, 'Do not go gentle into that good night', *Poems of Dylan Thomas*. New York: New Directions Publishing Co.; London: J. M. Dent & Sons Ltd, 1952. Copyright 1952 by Dylan Thomas. Reprinted by permission of New Directions Publishing Co. and David Higham Associates Ltd.

Edward Thomas, 'Words', lines 12–41, *Collected Poems*. London: Faber & Faber Ltd, 1979.

Lewis Thomas. *Late Night Thoughts on Listening to Mahler's Ninth Symphony*. New York: Viking Penguin Inc., 1983, pp. 167–8. Copyright © 1982 by Lewis Thomas. Reprinted by permission of the publisher.

Dickie Thompson. 'Thirteen Women' (recorded by Bill Haley, Decca Records DL/5027). Copyright © 1954 by Danby Music Company. By permission of Cinephonic Ltd and Danby Music Co.

Edward Thompson. *Beyond the Cold War*. London: Merlin Press Ltd, 1982, pp. 18–19, 35–6. Reprinted by permission of the author and publisher. *See also* Tsujimoto.

Henry Thoreau. 'On the Duty of Civil Disobedience', 'Walden', *Walden and Civil Disobedience*. New York: New American Library, 1980, pp. 226–31, 216, 155–7.

Thucydides. *The Peloponnesian War*, 3.82–3, trans. Thomas Hobbes.

The Times (London), 7, 8 August 1945, 3 June 1980, 5 September 1983. Reprinted by permission of the Editor.

Leo Tolstoy, *War and Peace*, part 10, XXV, trans. Constance Garnett, London: William Heinemann Ltd, 1971, p. 840. Reprinted by permission.

Cyril Tourneur. *The Atheist's Tragedy*, 2, 1.

Harry S. Truman, *see The Times*, 3 June 1980.

Fujio Tsujimoto. Quoted in Edward Thompson, *Protest and Survive*. London: CND, 1980, p. 14

Turkish Peace Association, *see* Furtado, *Turkey*.

United States National Security Council document NSC-68, 1950.

Vietnam veteran. Interview with Mike Wallace, CBS News. *See New York Times,* 25 November, 1969.

Peter Watson. *War on the Mind,* London: Hutchinson Publishing Group Ltd, 1980, pp. 181–2. Reprinted by permission.

James Watt, *see* Franklin, 'The Religious Right'.

Caspar Weinberger. *New York Times,* 23 August 1982.

H. G. Wells. 'The Red Room', *Tales of Wonder.* London: William Collins Sons Ltd, 1953, pp. 118–19. Reprinted by permission of the Trustees of the Estate of H. G. Wells.

H. G. Wells. 'The Country of the Blind', *Tales of Wonder.* London: Williams Collins Sons Ltd, 1953, pp. 235–42. Reprinted by permission of the Trustees of the Estate of H. G. Wells.

Rebecca West. *Black Lamb and Grey Falcon.* New York: Viking Penguin, Inc.; London: Macmillan Ltd, 1982, p. 1102. Copyright 1940, 1941 by Rebecca West. Copyright renewed © 1968, 1969 by Rebecca West. Reprinted by permission of A. D. Peters & Co. Ltd and Viking Penguin Inc.

Benjamin Lee Whorf. *Language, Thought, and Reality.* Cambridge, Mass.: The MIT Press, 1956. Reprinted by permission.

Kaiser Wilhelm. Quoted in Jerome D. Frank, 'The Nuclear Arms Race—Sociopsychological Aspects', *American Journal of Public Health,* 70 (1980), 950–2.

Susannah York. Speech in Trafalgar Square. Unpublished. Reprinted by permission of Susannah York.

Yuri Zhukov. Reprinted in END Special Report *Moscow Independent Peace Group,* ed. Jean Stead and Danielle Grunberg. London: Merlin Press Ltd, 1982. Reprinted by permission.

Faber and Faber Limited apologize for any errors or omissions in the above list of acknowledgements and would be grateful to be notified of any corrections that should be incorporated in the next edition of this volume.